THE KEY IDEAS OF MARTIN HEIDEGGER'S TREATISE **BEING AND TIME**

Walter Eisenbeis

UNIVERSITY
PRESS OF
AMERICA

Library of Congress Catalog Card Number: 82-23874

TO ALL THOSE OF MY STUDENTS WHO
ENTHUSIASTICALLY STUDIED
MARTIN HEIDEGGER's GREAT WORK
AND IN DOING SO
GAINED NEW INTELLECTUAL INSIGHT
FOR THEIR OWN LIVES

ACKNOWLEDGMENTS

My special thanks must be expressed to two persons: Mrs. Linda Payne who typed the whole English part of the book and the Rev. Paul Holbrook Jr, my friend and former student, who took it upon himself to work faithfully through the whole English portion of the book, smoothing out all the "Germanisms" which had been crept into it and correcting the various errors which he found

For errors which still are to be found I bear the responsibility. Should the reader still discover some I would be very pleased if this would be drawn to my attention for future corrections.

Denison University
Granville, Ohio
November 5, 1982   Walter Eisenbeis

INHALTSVERZEICHNIS

EINLEITUNG: DIE EXPOSITION DER FRAGE NACH DEM   4
        SINN VOM SEIN

  1. Notwendigkeit, Struktur und Vorrang   4
     der Seinsfrage
  2. Die Doppelaufgabe in der Ausarbeitung   8
     der Seinsfrage. Die Methode der Unter-
     suchung und ihr Aufriss

1. ABSCHNITT: DIE VORBEREITENDE FUNDAMENTAL-   18
        ANALYSE DES DASEINS

  1. Die Exposition der Aufgabe einer vorbe-   20
     reitenden Analyse des Daseins
  2. Das In-der-Welt-sein überhaupt als   24
     Grundverfassung des Daseins
  3. Die Weltlichkeit der Welt   26
  4. Das In-der-Welt-sein als Mit- und   42
     Selbstsein. Das "Man"
  5. Das In-Sein als solches   48
  6. Die Sorge als Sein des Daseins   64

2. ABSCHNITT: DASEIN UND ZEITLICHKEIT   84

  1. Das mögliche Ganzsein des Daseins und   86
     das Sein zum Tode
  2. Die daseinsmässige Bezeugung eines   98
     eigentlichen Seinkönnens und die
     Entschlossenheit
  3. Das eigentliche Ganzseinkönnen des   112
     Daseins und die Zeitlichkeit als der
     ontologische Sinn der Sorge
  4. Zeitlichkeit und Alltäglichkeit   124
  5. Zeitlichkeit und Geschichtlichkeit   136
  6. Zeitlichkeit und Innerzeitigkeit als   148
     Ursprung des vulgären Zeitbegriffes

TABLE OF CONTENTS

INTRODUCTION: EXPOSITION OF THE QUESTION OF   5
          THE MEANING OF BEING

   I.   The Necessity, Structure and Priority   5
       of the Question of Being
   II. The Twofold Task in Working out the   9
       Question of Being. Method and Design
       of our Investigation

DIVISION I: PREPARATORY FUNDAMENTAL ANALYSIS   19
            OF DASEIN

   I.   Exposition of the Task of a Prepara- 21
       tory Analysis of Dasein
   II. Being-in-the world in General as the 25
       Basic State of Dasein
   III. The Worldhood of the World   27
   IV. Being-in-the-world as Being-with and 43
       Being-one's-self. The "They"
   V.   Being-in as such   49
   VI. Care as the Being of Dasein   65

DIVISION II: DASEIN AND TEMPORALITY   85

   I.   Dasein's Possibility of Being-a-   87
       whole, and Being-towards-death
   II. Dasein's Attestation of an Authentic 99
       Potentiality-for-Being, and Resolute-
       ness
   III. Dasein's Authentic Potentiality-for- 113
       Being-a-whole, and Temporality as
       the Ontological Meaning of Care
   IV. Temporality and Everydayness   125
   V.   Temporality and Historicality   137
   VI. Temporality and Within-time-ness as 149
       the Source of the Ordinary Conception
       of Time

INTRODUCTION

This book attempts to list the key ideas which are contained in Martin Heidegger's famous philosophical treatise "Being and Time" [Sein und Zeit]. It does so by indicating for each paragraph a specific theme which Martin Heidegger discusses in the penetrating investigation of his existential analytic of Dasein.

In this way the structure of the whole work becomes accessible. This in turn shows how skillfully and carefully Martin Heidegger has written his first philosophical work of major proportions. It is hoped that this listing of the key ideas will help the reader to get a good picture of the work of an important philosopher of our century and also will facilitate the study of a treatise which has become a milestone in the history of philosophy, but one which is difficult to read.

For reasons of comparison and better comprehension of the English translation, as well as for those of accuracy and reference, all pages with even numbers give the key ideas in German, while the opposite pages with uneven numbers list the same key ideas in English. For the English text the excellent translation of "Sein und Zeit" ["Being and Time"] by John Macquarrie and Edward Robinson has been used.

On just a few occasions there is a difference in the setting up of the paragraphs between the original German edition [here the 10th edition is used] and the English translation. When a German paragraph has been broken up into two paragraphs in the English edition the latter are listed as "a" and "b". This is the case for paragraphs 55, 63, 196, 720, 747, 923, 955, and 1000. In three instances, paragraphs 754, 924, and 1228, the translators have united two paragraphs of the German edition to one in the English edition. This is indicated in the English edition by having these numbers in parentheses.

Martin Heidegger

SEIN UND ZEIT

BEING AND TIME

1

TRANSLATORS' PREFACE   (pp.13-16)

p.13   01. General remarks about Martin Heidegger's
          work "Being and Time"
       02. The goals of the translators
       03. The way in which Martin Heidegger employs
          the German language for his philosophical
          endeavors
p.14   04. The translators' method of translating the
          new special philosophical terms which Mar-
          tin Heidegger has employed
p.15   05. Reference to footnotes in which the trans-
          lators will discuss important terms of Mar-
          tin Heidegger's work
       06. The use of quotation marks, hyphenated ex-
          pressions, and italics
p.16   07. Acknowledgments to various persons and the
          German publisher
       08. Expression of thanks to the University of
          Kansas and the University of Kansas Endow-
          ment Association

       AUTHOR'S PREFACE TO THE SEVENTH
          GERMAN EDITION   (p.17)

p.17   1. The first appearance of "Being and Time"
       2. The 7th edition of this treatise
       3. About the planned continuation of "Being and
          Time"
       4. Further literature

       INTRODUCTORY REMARKS (p.19)

p.19   5. The question of the meaning of Being
       6. The necessity of introductory considerations
          for "Being and Time"

3

EINLEITUNG:
DIE EXPOSITION DER FRAGE NACH DEM
SINN VOM SEIN   (S.2-40)

Kapitel 1

NOTWENDIGKEIT, STRUKTUR UND VORRANG
DER SEINSFRAGE (S.2-15)

1. Die Notwendigkeit einer
ausdrücklichen Wiederholung der Frage
nach dem Sein (S.2-4)

S.2   7. Die Frage bei Plato und Aristoteles und ihr
            seitheriges Verstummen
         8. Das Dogma von der Überflüssigkeit der Frage
            nach dem Sein
         9. Methodische Erwägungen über Vorurteile gegen-
            über der Seinsfrage
S.3   10. Die drei Vorurteile gegenüber der Seinsfrage:
            1. Das Sein als allgemeiner Begriff
S.4   11. 2. Die Undefinierbarkeit des Begriffes "Sein"
        12. 3. Das Sein als selbstverständlichster Be-
            griff
        13. Das Problem der Selbstverständlichkeit philo-
            sophischer Begriffe
        14. Ergebnis der Erwägungen über die Vorurteile
            der Frage nach dem Sein

        2. Die formale Struktur der Frage
                nach dem Sein (S.5-8)

S.5   15. Methodische Erwägungen zur Stellung der Frage
            nach dem Sinn des Seins
        16. Strukturmomente und das Wesen des Fragens
        17. Das Stellen der Frage nach dem Sinn des Seins

4

INTRODUCTION:
EXPOSITION OF THE QUESTION OF THE
MEANING OF BEING (pp.21-64)

Chapter I

THE NECESSITY, STRUCTURE, AND PRIORITY
OF THE QUESTION OF BEING (pp.22-35)

1. The Necessity for Explicitly
Restating the Question of Being
(pp.22-24)

p.21   7. The question raised by Plato and Aristotle
            and its subsistence since that time
        8. The dogma that the question of Being is su-
            perfluous
        9. Methodical considerations about the pre-
            conceived concepts concerning the question
            of Being
p.22   10. The three pre-conceived concepts about the
            question of Being:
            1. Being as the most universal concept
p.23   11. 2. The inability to define the concept of
            Being
       12. 3. Being as the most self-evident concept
       13. The problem of the self-evidence with regard
            to philosophical concepts
p.24   14. The result of the considerations about pre-
            conceived concepts concerning the question
            of Being

2. The Formal Structure of the
Question of Being (pp.24-28)

p.24   15. Methodical considerations about postulating
            the question of the meaning of Being
       16. Structural elements and the nature of every
            inquiry
p.25   17. Postulating the question of the meaning of
            Being

5

S.5   18. Durchschnittliches und vages Seinsverständnis

19. Der ausgebildete Begriff vom Sein und das durchschnittliche Seinsverständnis

S.6   20. Überlieferungen von Theorien und Meinungen über das Sein

21. Das Sein als das Gefragte und der Sinn des Seins als das Erfragte

22. Das Problem des Seienden als des Befragten der Seinsfrage

S.7   23. Dasein als das für die Seinsfrage exemplarische Seiende

24. Erwägungen über den bisher versuchten methodischen Ansatz zur Seinsfrage: 1. Das Problem des Zirkels

25. 2. Das Sein als Voraussetzung und als Grund

S.8   26. Das Dasein und sein ausgezeichneter Bezug zur Frage des Seins

3. Der ontologische Vorrang der Seinsfrage (S.8-11)

S.8   27. Die Abgrenzung der Auszeichnung der Seinsfrage

28. Das Problem des Zwecks der Seinsfrage

S.9   29. Das Sein und die Wissenschaften als Sachgebiete des Seienden

30. Die Seinsfrage und die Grundbegriffe der Wissenschaft

31. Die heutigen Grundlagenkrisen (1926) einzelner Wissenschaften

S.10   32. Grundlegung der Wissenschaft als Auslegung des Seienden auf die Grundverfassung seines Seins hin, d.h. als Ontologie

S.11   33. Der Sinn des Seins als Vorverständigung des ontologischen Fragens

34. Apriorische Bedingungen der Möglichkeit der Ontologie als Ziel der Seinsfrage

35. Der ontologische Vorrang der Seinsfrage in der ontologischen Forschung

4. Der ontische Vorrang der Seinsfrage (S.11-15)

S.11   36. Wissenschaften und Dasein

6

p.25   18. The vague average understandung of Being
            as that which is given
        19. The explicit concept of Being and the aver-
            age understanding of Being
        20. Traditional theories and opinions about
            Being
        21. Being as that which is asked about and the
            meaning of Being as that which is to be
            found out by asking
p.26   22. The problem of entities as that which is in-
            terrogated as regards its Being
        23. Dasein as that entity which is exemplary
            for the question of Being
p.27   24. Considerations concerning the methodical
            disposition of the question of Being at-
            tempted thus far:
            1. The problem of circularity
        25. 2. Being as presupposition and as ground
p.28   26. Dasein and its very special relatedness to
            the question of Being

            3. The Ontological Priority of
            the Question of Being (pp.28-31)

p.28   27. Delimitation of the distinction of the
            question of Being
p.29   28. The problem of the purpose of the question
            of Being
        29. Being and the sciences as areas of subject
            matter concerning the entities
        30. The question of Being and the basic con-
            cepts of the sciences
        31. The present crisis (1926) in the foundations
            of individual sciences
p.30   32. Laying the foundations for the sciences as
            an interpretation of the constitution of
            their Being, i.e. as ontology
p.31   33. The meaning of Being as prior-understanding
            of ontological inquiry
        34. The a priori conditions for the possibility
            of ontology as the goal of the question of
            Being
        35. The ontological priority of the question of
            Being in ontological research

            4. The Ontical Priority of the
            Question of Being (pp.32-35)

p.32   36. Sciences and Dasein

S.12   37. Die Seinsverfassung des Daseins
        38. Vorontologisches Sein des Daseins
        39. Dasein und Existenz
        40. Existenzielles Verständnis und existenzia-
            les Verstehen
S.13   41. Existenzialität als Seinsverfassung des Sei-
            enden
        42. Dasein und Sein in einer Welt
        43. Existenziale Analytik des Daseins als Grund-
            lage der Fundamentalontologie
        44. Der ontologische Vorrang des Daseins vor
            allem anderen Seienden
        45. Der ontische Vorrang der Seinsfrage
S.14   46. Der ontisch-ontologische Vorrang des Daseins
            bei Aristoteles und Thomas von Aquino
        47. Die Fundamentalontologie als ontologische
            Analytik des Daseins
        48. Das Wesen der Seinsfrage

Kapitel 2

DIE DOPPELAUFGABE IN DER AUSARBEITUNG
DER SEINSFRAGE. DIE METHODE DER
UNTERSUCHUNG UND IHR AUFRISS   (S.15-40)

5. Die ontologische Analytik des
Daseins als Freilegung des Horizontes
für eine Interpretation des Sinnes
von Sein überhaupt (S.15-19)

S.15   49. Zusammenfassung über die Aufgabe der Stel-
            lung der Seinsfrage
        50. Rückstrahlung des Weltverhältnisses auf die
            Daseinsauslegung
S.16   51. Das Verdecktbleiben der dem Dasein spezifi-
            schen Seinsverfassung
        52. Die eigentümlichen Schwierigkeiten der In-
            terpretation des Daseins
        53. Methodische Erwägungen über die existenziale
            Analytik und den Reichtum der Ausgelegtheit
            des Daseins:
            1. Grundsätzliches
        54. 2. Alltäglichkeit als die Grundverfassung
            des Daseins

8

p.32   37. The constitution of Dasein's Being
        38. Pre-ontological Being of Dasein
        39. Dasein and existence
p.33   40. Existentiell understanding and understanding
            in terms of existentiality
        41. Existentiality as constitution of the Being
            of entities
        42. Dasein and Being in the world
p.34   43. Existential analytic of Dasein as foundation
            of fundamental ontology
        44. The priority of Dasein over all other enti-
            ties
        45. The ontical priority of the question of
            Being
        46. The ontico-ontological priority of Dasein
            as found in the works of Aristotle and
            Thomas Aquinas
        47. Fundamental ontology as ontological analytic
            of Dasein
p.35   48. The nature of the question of Being

Chapter II

THE TWOFOLD TASK IN WORKING OUT THE
QUESTION OF BEING. METHOD AND DESGIN
OF OUR INVESTIGATION (pp.36-64)

5. The Ontological Analytic of Dasein
   as Laying Bare the Horizon for an
   Interpretation of the Meaning of
      Being in General (pp.36-40)

p.36   49. Summary of the task of formulating the
            question of Being
        50. The way the world is understood and its
            reflecting back upon the interpretation
            of Dasein
p.37   51. The specific constitution of Dasein which
            remains concealed
        52. The peculiar difficulties of the inter-
            pretation of Dasein
        53. Methodical considerations about existential
            analytic and the richness according to which
            Dasein has been interpreted:
            1. Basic aspects
        54. 2. Everydayness as the basic state of Dasein

9

S.17   55. 3. Die Unvollständigkeit und Vorläufigkeit
            von Martin Heideggers Analyse des Daseins
        56. 4. Die Zeitlichkeit als Sinn des Daseins
        57. 5. Die Zeit als Horizont alles Seinsver-
            ständnisses und jeder Seinsauslegung
S.18   58. Zeit als Kriterium der Scheidung von Seins-
            regionen
        59. Die Aufgabe der Ontologie:
        60. 1. Die Temporalität des Seins
S.19   61. 2. Die Antwort auf die Frage der Temporali-
            tät des Seins als Leitfadenanweisung für
            die ontologische Forschung
        62. Bedingungen für die Antwort auf die Seins-
            frage

            6. Die Aufgabe einer Destruktion
        der Geschichte der Ontologie (S.19-27)

S.19   63. Das Kennzeichnende der elementaren Ge-
            schichtlichkeit des Daseins
S.20   64. Die Möglichkeit der Historizität als Seins-
            art des fragenden Daseins
        65. Die Frage nach dem Sinn des Seins als histo-
            rische Frage
S.21   66. Verfallensein des Daseins an die Welt
        67. Tradition und die Entwurzelung der Ge-
            schichtlichkeit des Daseins
        68. Das Problematische der bisherigen Geschich-
            te der Ontologie
S.22   69. Notwendigkeit der Destruktion des überlie-
            ferten Bestandes der antiken Philosophie
        70. Die positive Absicht dieser Destruktion
S.23   71. Methodische Erwägungen zur Ausarbeitung der
            Seinsfrage
        72. Kant und die Problematik der Temporalität
        73. Die Übersehung der ontologischen Bedeutsam-
            keit der Zeit bei Kant
S.24   74. Kants Abhängigkeit von Descartes und dessen
            Missverständnis der Seinsfrage
        75. Descartes Abhängigkeit von der mittelalter-
            lichen Ontologie der Scholastik
S.25   76. Die Tragweite der Nichtbestimmung der res
            cogitans bei Descartes
        77. Beispiele der Seinsauslegung aus der antiken
            Philosophie

p.38   55.a/b 3. The incompleteness and provisional
                  character of Martin Heidegger's a-
                  nalysis of Dasein
       56. 4. Temporality as the meaning of Dasein
p.39   57. 5. Time as the horizon for all understand-
                  ing of Being and for all interpretation
                  of Being
       58. Time as a criterion for discriminating
           realms of entities
p.40   59. The task of ontology:
       60. 1. The temporality of Being
       61. 2. The answer to the question of the tempo-
              rality of Being as providing the clues
              for ontological research
       62. Conditions for the answer given to the
           question of Being

           6. The Task of Destroying the
           History of Ontology (pp.41-49)

p.41   63.a/b The characteristics of the elemental
                  historicality of Dasein
       64. The possibility of historicity as the kind
           of Being inquiring Dasein
p.42   65. The inquiry into the meaning of Being as
           historical inquiry
       66. Dasein's falling back upon its world
p.43   67. Tradition and Dasein's being uprooted in
           its historicality
       68. The problematics concerning the approach of
           the study of the history of ontology
p.44   69. The necessity for destructing the tradition-
           al content of ancient ontology
       70. The positive intention of this destruction
       71. Methodical considerations concerning the
           working out of the question of Being
       72. Kant and the problematic of temporality
p.45   73. Kant's omission of the ontological
           significance of time
p.46   74. Kant's dependence upon Descartes and on
           Descartes' misunderstanding of the question
           of Being
       75. Descartes' dependence upon the medieval
           ontology of scholasticism
       76. The import of Descartes' neglect to deter-
           mine the res cogitans
p.47   77. Examples of the interpretation of Being
           in ancient philosophy

S.26   78. Die Problematik des antiken Zeitverständnisses
79. Methodische Erwägungen bezüglich der weiteren Untersuchung:
    1. Zum antiken Zeitbegriff
80. 2. Zu Aristoteles Abhandlung über die Zeit
81. 3. Zur Seinsfrage
82. 4. Zum Ergebnis dieser Erwägungen

7. Die phänomenologische Methode
   der Untersuchung (S.27-39)

S.27   83. Die Aufgabe der Ontologie
84. Abgrenzung von Wesen und Funktion der Ontologie
85. Phänomenologie als Methode für die Seinsfrage in der Ontologie
86. Phänomenologie als Maxime "zu den Sachen selbst"
S.28   87. Methodisches zum Vorbegriff der Phänomenologie

A. Der Begriff des Phänomens (S.28-31)

S.28   88. Das Wesen des Phänomens als das Sich-an-ihm-selbst-zeigende und seine Doppeldeutigkeit als Offenbarung und Schein
S.29   89. Die formale Grundstruktur des Erscheinens
90. Phänomene als Voraussetzung des Erscheinens
S.30   91. Die drei verschiedenen Bedeutungen von "Erscheinung"
92. Kants Gebrauch von "blosse Erscheinung"
93. Erscheinung als möglicher blosser Schein
S.31   94. Das Wesen des Phänomens und seine Abgrenzung gegenüber der Erscheinung
95. Der vulgäre Phänomenbegriff bei Kant und der formale Phänomenbegriff
96. Methodische Hinweise für die weitere Darstellung der phänomenologischen Methode

B. Der Begriff des Logos (S.32-34)

S.32   97. Logos und Urteil
98. Apophansis als Struktur des Logos

p.48   78. The problematic of the understanding of
           time as found in ancient philosophy
       79. Methodical considerations for the continua-
           tion of the study of Martin Heidegger's
           treatise concerning:
           1. The concept of time in ancient philosophy
       80. 2. Aristotle's treatise about time
       81. 3. The question of Being
       82. 4. The Summary of these methodical
           considerations

           7. The Phenomenological Method
              of Investigation (pp.49-63)

p.49   83. The task of ontology
       84. Delimitation of the nature and function of
           ontology
       85. Phenomenology as method for dealing with the
           question of Being in ontology
p.50   86. Phenomenology as maxim "To the things
           themselves"
       87. Methodical considerations about the prelim-
           inary conception of phenomenology

       A. The Concept of Phenomenon
               (pp.28-31)

p.51   88. The nature of the phenomenon as that which
           shows itself in itself and its double mean-
           ing as "manifest" and "semblance"
p.52   89. The basic formal structure of appearing
p.53   90. Phenomena as presupposition of appearing
       91. The three different meanings of "appearance"
       92. Kant's use of "mere appearance"
p.54   93. Appearance as possible mere semblance
       94. The nature of the phenomenon and its delim-
           itation concerning appearances
       95. The ordinary conception of phenomenon found
           in the work of Kant and the formal concep-
           tion of phenomenon
p.55   96. Methodical considerations about the continu-
           ing discussion of the phenomenological
           method

       B. The Concept of Logos
               (pp.32-34)

p.55   97. Logos and judgment
p.56   98. Apophansis as structure of the Logos

13

S.32   99. Sprechen als der konkrete Vollzug des
             Redens
S.33   100. Synthesis als Strukturform des Logos
       101. Logos und Aletheia -- Entdecken des Ver-
             borgenen als Wahrheit
       102. Aisthesis als primäre Wahrheit bei den
             Griechen
S.34   103. Die Urteilswahrheit
       104. Logos als Vernunft, Grund, Beziehung und
             Verhältnis
       105. Abschliessende Bemerkung über apophanti-
             sche Rede

       C. Der Vorbegriff der Phänomenologie
          (S.34-39)

S.34   106. Das Wesen der Phänomenologie
       107. Die Aufgabe der Phänomenologie
S.35   108. Das im ausgezeichneten Sinn Phänomen
             Seiende
       109. Das Sein des Seienden als Gegenstand der
             Phänomenologie
       110. Der Zusammenhang von Phänomenologie und
             Ontologie
S.36   111. Verdecktheit als Gegenbegriff zu Phänomen
       112. Verborgenheit, Verschüttung und Verstel-
             lung als die drei verschiedenen Arten der
             möglichen Verdecktheit der Phänomene
       113. "Zufällig" und "notwendig" als die zweifa-
             che Möglichkeit jeder Art der Verdecktheit
       114. Die Notwendigkeit eigener methodischer Si-
             cherung der Phänomenologie
S.37   115. Die Bedeutungen von "phänomenal" und von
             "phänomenologisch"
       116. Die Voraufgabe einer phänomenologischen
             Sicherung des exemplarischen Seienden als
             Ausgangspunkt für die eigentliche Analytik
       117. Phänomenologie als Ontologie und Hermeneu-
             tik als Phänomenologie des Daseins
S.38   118. Die Transzendenz des Seins des Daseins
       119. Philosophie als Ontologie und Phänomeno-
             logie
       120. Edmund Husserls Studien als Vorlage für
             Martin Heideggers Untersuchung
       121. Die Notwendigkeit aussergewöhnlicher
             sprachlicher Formulierungen für die Er-
             schliessung eines noch unbekannten Seins-
             gebietes

p.56   99. Speaking as fully concrete discoursing
       100. Synthesis as a structural form of the Logos
       101. Logos and Aletheia -- discovery of that
            which is hidden as truth
p.57   102. Aisthesis as primordial truth in the Greek
            conception of truth
       103. The truth of judgments
p.58   104. Logos as reason, ground, relation and
            relationship
       105. Closing remarks about apophantical discourse

       C. The Preliminary Conception
          of Phenomenology (pp.34-39)

p.58   106. The nature of phenomenology
       107. The task of phenomenology
p.59   108. The entities which are phenomena in a spe-
            cial meaning
       109. The Being of entities as the object of
            phenomenology
p.60   110. The interconnection between ontology and
            phenomenology
       111. Covered-up-ness as counter-concept to
            phenomenology
       112. Hiddenness, burying-over and disguise as the
            three accidental kinds of a possible
            covering-up of the phenomena
       113. "Accidental" and "necessary" as the twofold
            possibility of every kind of covering-up
p.61   114. The necessity of securing phenomenology as
            far as its own methods are concerned
       115. The signification of "phenomenal" and
            "phenomenological"
       116. The prior task of assuring ourselves
            phenomenologically of Dasein as that entity
            which is to serve as point of departure for
            the existential analysis
       117. Phenomenology as ontology and hermeneutic
            as phenomenology of Dasein
p.62   118. The transcendence of Dasein's Being
       119. Philosophy as ontology and phenomenology
       120. The studies of Edmund Husserl as preparation
            for Martin Heidegger's treatise
p.63   121. The necessity for the harshness of expres-
            sion with regard to the opening-up of a
            still unknown realm of Being

8. Der Aufriss der Abhandlung
(S.39-40)

1. Teil:

Die Interpretation des Daseins auf die
Zeitlichkeit und die Explikation der
Zeit als des transzendentalen
Horizontes der Frage nach dem Sein

(S.41-437)

1. Abschnitt:

DIE VORBEREITENDE FUNDAMENTALANALYSE
DES DASEINS

(S.41-230)

S.41   124. Einleitung und Gliederung des 1. Ab-
        schnittes

18

Part 1

The Interpretation of Dasein in Terms of
Temporality, and the Explication of Time
as the Transcendental Horizon for the
Question of Being

(pp.65-488)

Division I

PREPARATORY FUNDAMENTAL ANALYSIS OF DASEIN

(pp.65-273)

19

Kapitel 1

DIE EXPOSITION DER AUFGABE EINER
VORBEREITENDEN ANALYSE DES DASEINS
(S.41-52)

9. Das Thema der Analytik des Daseins
(S.41-45)

S.41   125. Die Charakteristik des Daseins
S.42   126. Die beiden Charaktere des Daseins:
             1. Das Zu-sein:
                a) Vorhandensein und Vorhandenheit
        127.   b) Der Vorrang der Existenz vor der
                   Essenz
        128. 2. Jemeinigkeit:
                a) Jemeinigkeit als bestimmendes Element
                   des Daseins
        129.   b) Eigentlichkeit und Uneigentlichkeit
                   als die Seinsmodi des Daseins
S.43   130. Das Problem der möglichen Vorgegebenheit
             des Daseins
        131. Die alltägliche Indifferenz des Daseins als
             seine Durchschnittlichkeit
        132. Die Notwendigkeit der Postulierung der
             durchschnittlichen Alltäglichkeit des Da-
             seins
S.44   133. Die durchschnittliche Alltäglichkeit des Da-
             seins und das a priori der Struktur der
             Existenzialität
        134. Durchschnittliche Alltäglichkeit des Da-
             seins und ontologische Strukturen
        135. Existenzialien und Kategorien als Grundmög-
             lichkeiten von Seinscharakteren
S.45   136. Die Vorrangstellung der existenzialen Ana-
             lytik des Daseins

10. Die Abgrenzung der Daseinsanalytik
gegen Anthropologie, Psychologie
und Biologie (S.45-50)

S.45   137. Die ontologische Frage als Grundlage für
             die Abgrenzung
        138. Descartes Ausserachtlassen des sum
S.46   139. Methodische Erwägungen über die Idee von
             "Subjekt"
        140. Die Vernachlässigung des Problems des Da-
             seins in der Lebensphilosophie

20

Chapter I

EXPOSITION OF THE TASK OF A PREPARATORY
ANALYSIS OF DASEIN (pp.67-77)

9. The Theme of the Analytic
of Dasein (pp.67-71)

p.67 125. The characteristic of Dasein
      126. The two characters of Dasein:
           1. The "to be":
              a) Being-present-at-hand and presence-
                 at-hand
      127.   b) The priority of "existentia" over
                 "essentia"
      128. 2. Mineness:
              a) Mineness as the determining element
                 of Dasein
p.68 129.   b) Authenticity and inauthenticity as
                 modes of Dasein's Being
      130. The problem of the possible giveness of
           Dasein
p.69 131. The every-day undifferentiated character of
           Dasein as its averageness
      132. The necessity of postulating Dasein's
           average everydayness
      133. Average everydayness of Dasein and the a
           priori of the structure of existentiality
p.70 134. Average everydayness of Dasein and
           ontological structures
      135. Existentialia and categories as basic
           possibilities of characters of Being
p.71 136. The priority of the existential analytic
           of Dasein

10. How the Analytic of Dasein is
to be Distinguished from Anthro-
pology, Psychology, and Biology
(pp.71-76)

p.71 137. The ontological question as a basis for the
           distinction in section 10
      138. Descartes' omission of the sum
      139. Methodical considerations about the idea of
           "subject"
p.72 140. The "philosophy of life" and its disregard-
           ing the problem of Dasein

21

S.46 141. Das Personsein als Aspekt philosophischer
           Anthropologie in der Philosophie von Dil-
           they, Bergson, Husserl und Scheler
S.47 142. Das Problematische dieses anthropologi-
           schen Ansatzes
S.48 143. Das Kennzeichnende der traditionellen An-
           thropologie und ihre relevanten Ursprünge:
           1. Die griechische Definition -- der
              Mensch als vernünftiges Lebewesen
      144. 2. Der theologische Leitfaden -- der
              Mensch als Ebenbild Gottes
S.49 145. Die Unbestimmtheit der entscheidenden onto-
           logischen Fundamente der Anthropologie
      146. Die Unbestimmtheit der entscheidenden onto-
           logischen Fundamente in Psychologie und
           Biologie
S.50 147. Anthropologie, Psychologie, Biologie und
           die ontologischen Fundamente dieser Wissen-
           schaften

      11. Die existenziale Analytik und die
      Interpretation des primitiven Daseins.
      Die Schwierigkeiten der Gewinnung
      eines "natürlichen" Weltbegriffes.
                (S.50-52)

S.50 148. Alltäglichkeit des Daseins und primitives
           Dasein
S.51 149. Die Ethnologie und ihre Bereitstellung der
           Kenntnis der archaischen Völker
S.52 150. Die Notwendigkeit der begrifflichen Ausar-
           beitung des Weltphänomens
      151. Der Zweck der Darlegungen in Abschnitt 11

22

p.72   141. "Personal Being" as aspect of the philosoph-
            ical anthropology in the philosophies of
            Dilthey, Bergson, Husserl and Scheler
p.73   142. The problematics of these anthropological
            points of departure
p.74   143. The characteristic of traditional anthropol-
            ogy and its relevant origins:
            1. The Greek definition -- the human person
               as something living which has reason
       144. 2. The theological clue -- the human person
               as the image of God
p.75   145. The lack of determination concerning the
            decisive ontological foundations of present
            anthropology
       146. The lack of determination concerning the
            decisive ontological foundations in present
            psychology and biology
       147. Anthropology, psychology, biology and the
            ontological foundations of these sciences

            11.   The Existential Analytic and
            the Interpretation of Primitive
            Dasein.   The Difficulties of
            Achieving a 'Natural Conception
            of the World' (pp.76-77)

p.76   148. Everydayness of Dasein and "primitive"
            Dasein
       149. Ethnology and our enrichment by it as it
            gives us knowledge about archaic peoples
       150. The necessity to conceptually work out the
            phenomenon of the world
p.77   151. The purpose of the considerations in section
            11.

Kapitel 2

DAS IN-DER-WELT-SEIN ÜBERHAUPT ALS
GRUNDVERFASSUNG DES DASEINS   (S.52-62)

12. Die Vorzeichnung des
In-der-Welt-seins aus der Orientierung
des In-Seins als solchem (S.52-59)

S.52   152. Zusammenfassung über die Seinsbestimmung
des Daseins
S.53   153. Methodische Erwägungen über Dasein als In-
der-Welt-sein
154. Das einheitliche Phänomen des In-der-Welt-
seins
155. Die konstitutiven Strukturmomente der Seinsverfassung des Daseins als dreifache Hin-
blicknahme auf das In-der-Welt-sein:
1. Die Idee der Weltlichkeit
156. 2. Das Seiende, das in der Weise des In-
der-Welt-seins ist
157. 3. Das In-Sein als solches
158. Das In-Sein als Kategorie
S.54   159. Das In-Sein als Existenzial
160. Methodische Erwägungen über "Sein bei" der
Welt als im In-Sein fundiertes Existenzial
S.55   161. "Sein bei" der Welt als Existenzial und die
Faktizität des Daseins
S.56   162. Der ontologische Unterschied zwischen dem
In-Sein als Existenzial und der "Inwendig-
keit" von Vorhandenem untereinander als
Kategorie
163. Die Mannigfaltigkeit der Weisen des In-
seins als die Seinsart des Besorgens
S.57   164. Dasein, Beziehungen zur Welt und In-der-
Welt-sein
165. Umwelt-haben und die Priorität des In-der-
Welt-seins
S.58   166. Der Charakter des phänomenologischen Aufwei-
ses des In-der-Welt-seins
167. Das Problematische des Welterkennens aus
der voraussetzenden Annahme einer Subjekt-
Objekt-Beziehung
S.59   168. Die "Modalität" des In-Seins

24

Chapter II

BEING-IN-THE-WORLD IN GENERAL AS THE
BASIC STATE OF DASEIN (pp.78-90)

12. A Preliminary Sketch of
Being-in-the-world, in
terms of an Orientation
towards Being-in as such
(pp.78-86)

p.78   152. Summary about the ways in which Dasein's
            Being takes on a definite Character
       153. Methodical considerations about Dasein as
            Being-in-the-world
       154. The unitary phenomenon of Being-in-the-world
       155. The constitutive structural items of Dasein's
            state of Being as the three ways of looking
            at Being-in-the-world:
            1. The idea of worldhood
p.79   156. 2. That entity which in every case has
               Being-in-the-world as the way in which
               it is
       157. 3. Being-in as such
       158. Being-in as category
       159. Being-in as existentiale
p.80   160. Methodical considerations about "Being
            alongside" as an existentiale founded upon
            Being-in
p.81   161. "Being alongside" as existentiale and as
            Dasein's facticity
p.82   162. The ontological difference between Being-in
            as existentiale and the category of
            "insideness" which things present-at-hand
            can have with regard to one another
p.83   163. The multiplicity of the ways of Being-in
            as the mode of concern
p.84   164. Dasein, relationship-of-Being-towards the
            world and Being-in-the-world
       165. Having an environment and the priority of
            Being-in-the-world
p.85   166. The character of the phenomenological way of
            exhibiting Being-in-the-world
       167. The problematics of knowing the world by
            presupposing a subject-object-relationship
p.86   168. The existential "modality" of Being-in

25

<u>13. Die Exemplifizierung des In-Seins</u>
<u>an einem fundierten Modus.</u>
<u>Das Welterkennen</u> (S.59-62)

S.59 169. Dasein und Welt und ihre Beziehung zur üb-
          lichen Erkenntnistheorie
S.60 170. Das Problematische der üblichen auf der Sub-
          jekt-Objekt-Beziehung aufbauenden Erkennt-
          nistheorie
S.61 171. Erkennen als eine Seinsart des In-der-Welt-
          seins und das Erkenntnisproblem
      172. Das Wesen des vorgängigen Gründens des Er-
          kennens in dem Schon-bei-der-Welt-sein --
          der Fundierungszusammenhang der für das
          Welterkennen konstitutiven Modi des In-der-
          Welt-seins
S.62 173. "Innen" und "aussen" in der Verbindung mit
          dem In-der-Welt-sein
      174. Zusammenfassung über das Erkennen als ein
          im In-der-Welt-sein fundierter Modus des
          Daseins

Kapitel 3

DIE WELTLICHKEIT DER WELT (S.63-113)

<u>14. Die Idee der Weltlichkeit</u>
<u>der Welt überhaupt</u> (S.63-66)

S.63 175. Methodische Erwägungen über das Strukturmo-
          ment "Welt"
      176. Naturdinge und Substanzialität
      177. Natur als innerhalb der Welt begegnendes
          Seiendes
      178. Wertbehaftete Dinge als innerhalb der Welt
          begegnendes Seiendes
S.64 179. Welt als Voraussetzung in den Zugangsarten
          zum "objektiven Sein"
      180. Methodische Erwägungen über die phänomeno-
          logische Angehung des Problems "Welt"
      181. Weltlichkeit von Welt als Existenzial
      182. <u>Die Vieldeutigkeit des Wortes "Welt":</u>
      183. <u>1. Als ontischer Begriff</u>
      184. 2. Als ontologischer Terminus
S.65 185. 3. Die vorontologisch existenzielle Bedeu-
          tung von Welt
      186. 4. Der ontologisch-existenziale Begriff
          "Weltlichkeit"

13. A Founded Mode in which Being-in is Exemplified Knowing the World
(pp.86-90)

p.86 169. Dasein and world and their relationship to the customary theory of knowledge

p.87 170. The problematics of the customary epistemology which is based upon a subject-object-relationship

p.88 171. Knowing as a mode of Dasein's Being as Being-in-the-world and the problem of cognition

172. The nature of the founding of knowing beforehand in a Being-already-alongside-the-world -- the modes of Being-in-the-world which are constitutive for knowing the world

p.89 173. "Inside" and "outside" in relation to Being-in-the-world

p.90 174. Summary about knowing as a mode of Dasein which is founded upon Being-in-the-world

Chapter III

THE WORLDHOOD OF THE WORLD
(pp.91-148)

14. The Idea of the Worldhood of the World in General (pp.91-95)

p.91 175. Methodical considerations about the structural item "world"

176. Things of Nature and substantiality

p.92 177. Nature as an entity which is encountered within the world

178. Things invested with value as entities which are encountered within the world

179. The world as a presupposition in the ways of access to "objective Being"

180. Methodical considerations about the phenomenological avenue leading to the problem "world"

181. The worldhood of the world as existentiale

p.93 182. The various ways of using the word "world":

183. 1. As ontical concept

184. 2. As ontological term

185. 3. The pre-ontological meaning of "world"

186. 4. As ontologico-existential concept of worldhood

S.65 187. Terminologische Abgrenzung von "weltlich"
             und "weltzugehörig" bzw. "innerweltlich"
      188. Natur und Weltlichkeit
      189. Die ontologische Analyse der Weltlichkeit
             und die überlieferte Ontologie
S.66 190. Methodische Erwägungen über Alltäglichkeit
             als Ausgangspunkt der ontologischen Analyse
             der Weltlichkeit
      191. Umwelt und Räumlichkeit des Daseins

A. DIE ANALYSE DER UMWELTLICHKEIT UND
   WELTLICHKEIT ÜBERHAUPT (S.66-89)

     15. Das Sein des in der Umwelt
    begegnenden Seienden (S.66-72)

S.66 192. Methodische Erwägungen über die Behandlung
             der Seinsart des besorgenden Umgangs
S.67 193. Die Seinsart des besorgenden Umgangs als
             phänomenologischer Zugang zu dem Gebrauch-
             ten und dem in Herstellung Befindlichen
      194. Dinge und das im Besorgen begegnende Sei-
             ende
S.68 195. Das Zeug als Bezeichnung des im Besorgen
             begegnenden Seienden
      196. Das Wesen des Zeugs -- Zeughaftigkeit als
             Zugehörigkeit zu einem Zeugganzen
S.69 197. Der auf das Zeug zugeschnittene Umgang --
             Zuhandenheit und Umsicht
      198. Der Unterschied von praktischem und theo-
             retischem Verhalten
      199. Das Zuhandene und das Werk
S.70 200. Das Werk und die ihm wesenhaft zugehörige
             Verwendbarkeit als das Wozu des Werkes
      201. Werk und Hinweis auf Materialien -- Natur
             und gebrauchtes Zeug
      202. Entdeckung der Umwelt als Entdeckung der
             Natur -- Entdeckung als das Woraus des Be-
             stehens des Werkes
      203. Das Werk und seine Verweisung auf den Trä-
             ger und Benutzer -- Entdeckung von öffent-
             licher Welt und Umweltnatur
S.71 204. Das Wesen der Zuhandenheit

28

p.93 187. Terminological delimitation of "worldly" and
           "belonging to the world" or "within-the-
           world"
      188. Nature and worldhood
p.94 189. The ontological analysis of worldhood and
           the traditional ontology
      190. Methodical considerations about everydayness
           as point of departure for the ontological
           analysis of worldhood
      191. Environment and Dasein's spatiality

           A. ANALYSIS OF ENVIRONMENTALITY AND
           WORLDHOOD IN GENERAL (pp.95-122)

           15. The Being of the Entities
           Encountered in the Environ-
                ment (pp.95-102)

p.95 192. Methodical considerations about the mode of
           concernful dealings
      193. The mode of concernful dealings as phenom-
           enological access to those entities which
           are used or which are to be found in the
           course of production
p.96 194. Things and those entities which are encoun-
           tered in concern
      195. Equipment as those entities which we encoun-
           ter in concern
p.97 196./196a. The nature of equipment --equipmental-
           ity as that which belongs to a totality
           of equipment
p.98 197. Dealings cut to the measure of equipment --
           readiness-to-hand and circumspection
p.99 198. The difference between practical and
           theoretical behavior
      199. The ready-to-hand and the work
      200. The work and the usability of the work's
           "towards which" that belongs to it
           essentially
      201. Work and reference to "materials" -- Nature
           and equipment that is used
p.100 202. The discovery of the environment as the dis-
           covery of Nature -- the discovery of the
           "whereof" of which the work consists
      203. The work and its reference to wearers and
           users -- the discovery of public world and
           of environing nature
p.101 204. The nature of the readiness-to-hand

29

S.72 205. Das Problem der ontologischen Fundierung
des Weltphänomens

16. Die am innerweltlich Seienden sich
meldende Weltmässigkeit der Umwelt
(S.72-76)

S.72 206. Das Problem des vorontologischen Verständnisses von Welt
207. Methodische Erwägungen über den Zugang zum
Phänomen der Welt
S.73 208. Auffallen als Stossen auf ein Unverwendba-
res innerhalb eines je schon Zuhandenen
209. Aufdringlichkeit als Bemerken des Unzuhan-
denen seitens des Zuhandenen
210. Aufsässigkeit als Unzuhandenes in der Weise
des Nichthergehörigen bzw. des Unerledigten
S.74 211. Die Funktion der Modi der Auffälligkeit,
Aufdringlichkeit und Aufsässigkeit als mo-
difiziertes Begegnen des Zuhandenen -- die
Weise des Begegnens des Zuhandenen, in der
sich seine Vorhandenheit enthüllt
212. Methodische Erwägungen über das Begegnen
des Zuhandenen und die Aufklärung des Weltphänomens
213. Auffälligkeit, Aufdringlichkeit, Aufsässigkeit und ihre Beziehung zu dem Zuhandenen
214. Der Zeugzusammenhang als Weg zur Welt
S.75 215. Erschliessen und Erschlossenheit als Auf-
schliessen und Aufgeschlossenheit
216. Die phänomenale Struktur des An-sich-seins
und die Welt
217. Unauffälligkeit, Unaufdringlichkeit und Un-
aufsässigkeit als phänomenale Charaktere
des Seins des zunächst Zuhandenen
S.76 218. Innerweltlich Zuhandenes und Erschlossensein
der Welt
219. Zusammenfassung der bisherigen Interpretation über das In-der-Welt-sein
220. Methodische Erwägungen zum Phänomen und zum
Problem der Weltlichkeit

p.101 205. The problem of the ontological founding of
          the phenomenon of the world

          16. How the Worldly Character of the
              Environment Announces itself in
                 Entities Within-the-world
                       (pp.102-107)

p.102 206. The problem of the pre-ontological under-
          standing of "world"
      207. Methodical considerations about the access
          to the phenomenon of the world
      208. Conspicuousness as coming up against unuse-
          able things within that which is ready-to-
          hand already
p.103 209. Obstrusiveness as noticing what is un-ready-
          to-hand by that which is ready-to-hand
      210. Obstinacy as that which is un-ready-to-hand
          in a manner of what does not belong here or
          of what has not as yet been attended to
p.104 211. The function of the modes of conspicuousness,
          obstrusiveness, and obstinacy as encounter-
          ing the ready-to-hand under modifications --
          the manner of the ready-to-hand in which its
          presence-at-hand is revealed
      212. Methodical considerations about the encoun-
          tering of the ready-to-hand and the explain-
          ing of the phenomenon of the world
      213. Conspicuousness, obstrusiveness, obstinacy
          and their relationship to the ready-to-hand
p.105 214. The context of equipment as way to the world
      215. "To disclose" and "disclosedness" as "to lay
          open" and "the character of having been
          laid open"
p.106 216. The phenomenal structure of Being-in-itself
          and the world
      217. Inconspicuousness, unobstrusiveness, and
          non-obstinacy as phenomenal characters of
          the Being of that which is proximally
          ready-to-hand
      218. The ready-to-hand within-the-world and
          disclosedness of the world
p.107 219. Summary of the previous interpretation of
          Being-in-the-world
      220. Methodical considerations about the phenom-
          enon and the problem of worldhood

31

17. Verweisung und Zeichen (S.76-83)

S.76 221. Zusammenfassung über das Sichtbarwerden des
           Phänomens der Verweisung bei der vorläufi-
           gen Interpretation der Zeuge als der Seins-
           struktur des Zuhandenen
S.77 222. Methodische Erwägungen über die Bestimmung
           des Phänomens der Verweisung
      223. Zeichen als Zeuge mit dem Charakter des Zei-
           gens und Verweisen als Beziehung
      224. Der formal-allgemeine Charakter der Bezie-
           hung
      225. Mannigfaltigkeit und Abgrenzung möglicher
           Zeichen
S.78 226. Die Signalanlage am Kraftwagen als exempla-
           risches Beispiel für das Zeichen
      227. Verweisung als Zeichen und als Dienlichkeit
S.79 228. Umsichtiges Übersehen als angemessene Um-
           gangsart mit Zeigzeug und als Weg zum Ver-
           stehen des Zeigens eines Zeichens
      229. Das Zeichen als ausdrückliche Übersicht im
           Sinne der Gewinnung einer Orientierung in-
           nerhalb der Umwelt
S.80 230. Die Zeichenstiftung als eigentlicher Zeug-
           charakter der Zeichen:
           1. Herstellung eines überhaupt noch nicht
           zuhandenen Zeugs
      231. 2. Das Zum-Zeichen-nehmen eines schon Zuhan-
           denen
S.81 232. Vorhandenes, Zeichen, Dinglichkeit
      233. Die verschiedenen Horizonte des Verstehens
           beim Zeichen
      234. Zusammenfallen von Zeichen und Gezeigtem im
           archaischen Denken -- Fetisch und Zauber
S.82 235. Zusammenfassung über die Beziehung zwischen
           Zeichen und Verweisung

18. Bewandtnis und Bedeutsamkeit;
die Weltlichkeit der Welt (S.83-88)

S.83 236. Zuhandenheit und Weltlichkeit
      237. Bewandtnis als Seinscharakter der Zuhanden-
           heit und Verwiesenheit als Struktur dieses
           Seins

32

17. <u>Reference and Signs</u>
(pp.107-114)

p.107 221. Summary about the phenomenon of reference or assignment which became visible in the provisional Interpretation as the structure of Being which belongs to the ready-to-hand

222. Methodical considerations about defining the phenomenon of reference or assignment

p.108 223. Signs as items of equipment with the character of indicating and referring as relating

224. The formally general character of relations

225. Multiplicity and delimitation of possible signs

226. The signal-lights of the motor car as an example for the sign

p.109 227. Referring as indicating and as having serviceability for

p.110 228. Circumspective survey as appropriate dealing with equipment for indicating and as a way of the understanding of the sign's indicating

229. The sign as an explicit survey in the sense of gaining an orientation within the environment

p.111 230. <u>Establishing a sign as peculiar character of signs as equipment:</u>
1. The producing of equipment which is not yet ready-to-hand

231. 2. The "taking as a sign" of something that is ready-to-hand

p.112 232. The present at hand, the sign, and thinghood

233. The sign and its various horizons with regard to understanding

234. Coinciding of the sign with that which is indicated in the horizon or archaic thinking -- fetishism and magic

p.113/114 235./235a. Summary of the relationship between sign and reference

18. <u>Involvement and Significance;</u>
<u>the Worldhood of the World</u>
(pp.114-122)

p.114 236. Readiness-to-hand and worldhood

237. Involvement as the character of Being of readiness-to-hand and that which has been assigned or referred as structure of this Being

33

S.84 238. Der Zusammenhang von Struktur der Bewandt-
nis und dem Sein des Daseins

239. Ontische und ontologische Bedeutung von Bewendenlassen

S.85 240. Der Charakter des ontologisch verstandenen
Bewendenlassens

241. Der ontologische Bezug zur Welt in der vor-
entdeckten Bewandtnisganzheit

242. Verstehen von In-der-Welt-sein als wesen-
hafter Bestand des Seinsverständnisses des
Daseins

S.86 243. Das Phänomen der Welt, die Weltlichkeit und
das Dasein

244. Weltvertrautheit des Daseins als Grund der
Möglichkeit ontologisch-existenzialer In-
terpretation des vorgängigen Verstehens im
Modus des Sichverweisens

245. Methodische Erwägungen über die weitere Erläuterung des Zusammenhanges vom Sichverwei-
sen des Daseins

S.87 246. Bedeutsamkeit als Struktur der Welt -- die
Angewiesenheit des Daseins auf eine ihm je
begegnende Welt

247. Bedeutsamkeit als ontologische Bedingung
für das Erschliessen von Bedeutung

248. Erschlossene Bedeutsamkeit als existenziale
Verfassung des Daseins

249. Das Problem der Weltlichkeit als das eines
Verweisungszusammenhanges

S.88 250. Zusammenfassung und Klärung des Unterschie-
des der Strukturen und Dimensionen der ontologischen Problematik bezüglich des bisherigen Untersuchungsfelds von Heideggers
Studie

251. Methodische Erwägungen zum folgenden Abschnitt B

B. DIE ABHEBUNG DER ANALYSE DER
WELTLICHKEIT GEGEN DIE INTERPRETATION
DER WELT BEI DESCARTES (S.89-101)

S.89 252. Methodische Erwägungen zur Diskussion der
Grundzüge der Ontologie der Welt bei Descartes

253. Gliederung der folgenden Analyse von Descartes ontologischem Ansatz

p.116 238. The interconnection between the structure of involvement and Dasein's Being

p.117 239. The ontical and ontological meaning of "letting something be involved"

240. The ontologically understood character of "letting something be involved"

p.118 241. The ontological relationship to the world in the prior discovery of a totality of involvements

242. Understanding of Being-in-the-world as essential content of Dasein's understanding of Being

243. The phenomenon of the world, worldhood, and Dasein

p.119 244. Dasein's familiarity with the world as the basis for the possibility for an ontologico-existential Interpretation with regard to Dasein's understanding of itself beforehand in the mode of assigning itself

p.120 245. Methodical considerations about further explanations of the interconnection of Dasein's assigning itself

246. Significance as structure of the world -- Dasein's submission to the world which it itself already encounters

p.121 247. Significance as ontological condition for the disclosedness of significations

248. Disclosed significance as existential state of Dasein

249. The problem of worldhood as that of a context of assignments and references

250. Summary and elucidation of the differences concerning the structures and dimensions of the ontological problematics within the present field of investigating Heidegger's treatise

p.122 251. Methodical considerations with regard to section B

B. A CONTRAST BETWEEN OUR ANALYSIS OF WORLDHOOD AND DESCARTES' INTERPRE-TATION OF THE WORLD (pp.122-134)

p.122 252. Methodical considerations about the discussion of the basic features of Descartes' ontology of the world

253. Organization of the analysis of Descartes' ontological point of departure

19. Die Bestimmung der Welt
als res extensa (S.89-92)

S.89   254. Die Doppeldeutigkeit von substantia bei
             Descartes
S.90   255. Ausdehnung als Charakterisierung der Sub-
             stanzialität der "Welt" bei Descartes
        256. Die Identität des Körperdinges bei Des-
             cartes
S.91   257. Das Charakteristische der Substanzialität
             eines Körperdinges bei Descartes

20. Die Fundamente der ontologischen
Bestimmung der "Welt" (S.92-95)

S.92   258. Substanzialität bei Descartes als Unbedürf-
             tigkeit eines Seienden
S.93   259. Descartes Übergehen der Frage nach dem Sinn
             des Seins
S.94   260. Die res extensa als die ontologische Grund-
             lage der "Welt" bei Descartes
        261. Die Doppeldeutigkeit der Substanz als Kenn-
             zeichen der Nichtbewältigung des grundsätz-
             lichen Seinsproblems bei Descartes

21. Die hermeneutische Diskussion
der cartesischen Ontologie der "Welt"
(S.95-101)

S.95   262. Methodische Vorüberlegung zu dem ontologi-
             schen Ansatz bei Descartes
        263. Die ontologische Fehlbestimmung der Welt
             bei Descartes auf Grund der Identifikation
             des Seins mit ständiger Vorhandenheit
S.96   264. Denken bei Descartes als eine durch die An-
             schauung fundierte Vollzugsform
        265. Descartes Wissen um das Unvermögen der Sin-
             ne, Seiendes in seinem Sein zu erkennen
S.97   266. Die Notwendigkeit der Erläuterung von
             Descartes problematischem Ansatz
        267. Descartes fragwürdige Interpretation der
             Härte als Widerstand
        268. Descartes fragwürdige Erörterung der mögli-
             chen Zugänge zum innerweltlich Seienden

19. The Definition of the "World" as res extensa (pp.123-125)

P.123 254. The ambiguity of Descartes' use of substantia

255. Descartes' characterization of the substantiality of the world as extension

p.124 256. Descartes' idea of the identity of the corporeal Thing

257. Descartes' idea of the characteristics of the substantiality of a corporeal Thing

20. Foundations of the Ontological Definition of the "World" (pp.125-127)

p.125 258. Descartes' idea of substantiality as an entity not needing anything

p.126 259. Descartes' evading of the inquiry into the meaning of Being

260. Descartes' idea of the res extensa as the ontological basis of the "world"

p.127 261. Descartes' ambiguity in his usage of substance as mark of his inability to deal adequately with the fundamental problem of Being

21. Hermeneutical Discussion of the Cartesian Ontology of the "World" (pp.128-134)

p.128 262. Preliminary methodical considerations about Descartes' ontological point of departure

263. Descartes' defective ontological conception of the world and the identification of Being with presence-at-hand as its basis

p.129 264. Descartes' idea that thinking ist just a more fully achieved form of beholding

265. Descartes' knowing that senses do not enable us to cognize any entity in its Being

p.130 266. The necessity of explaining the problematical point of departure in Descartes' epistemology

267. Descartes' dubious interpretation of hardness as resistance

268. Descartes' dubious explanation of the possible kinds of access to entities within-the-world

37

S.98 269. Gründe für die Fragwürdigkeit der cartesi-
schen Idee vom Sein als beständiger Vorhandenheit und als Substanz
270. War Descartes überhaupt an einer Ontologie
interessiert?
271. Descartes ontologisches Anliegen und die
Tatsache, dass er es verfehlte
272. Vermeintliche Argumente für Descartes
Grundlegung der ontologischen Charakteristik des innerweltlich Seienden als mate-
rieller Natur
S.99 273. Das ontologisch Problematische bei Dingontologie und Wertprädikaten
S.100 274. Dingontologie bei Descartes und Versuche,
sie zu ergänzen
275. Das Überspringen der Welt als ein in der
Seinsart des Daseins Gegründet-sein
276. Kritische Fragen bezüglich der Weltontologie von Descartes
277. Methodische Erwägungen zum Zugang zu dem
positiven Verständnis der Problematik der
Welt
S.101 278. Kritik an Descartes Weltontologie als Vorbereitung auf Heideggers Ansatz der Ontologie des Daseins
279. Die Bedeutsamkeit der extensio bei Descartes

C. DAS UMHAFTE DER UMWELT UND DIE
RÄUMLICHKEIT DES DASEINS (S.101-113)

S.101 280. Einleitende methodische Erwägungen über den
Zugang zur Räumlichkeit des Daseins und
über die Raumbestimmtheit der Welt

22. Die Räumlichkeit des
innerweltlich Zuhandenen (S.102-104)

S.102 281. Methodische Erwägungen über den Zusammenhang von Raum, Welt und Zuhandenem
282. Entfaltung des Verstehens der Charakteristik des Zuhandenen und seiner Beziehung
zum Räumlichen -- Nähe, Platz, das Hingehö-
ren eines Zeugs, die Gegend
S.103 283. Charakterisierung von Gegend als Richtung
und Umkreis

p.130 269. Reasons for the dubiousness of the idea of
          Being as permanent presence-at-hand and as
          substance
p.131 270. Was Descartes at all interested in ontology?
      271. Descartes' ontological interest and his
          missing of a primordial ontological
          problematic of Dasein
      272. Presumptive arguments in favor of Descartes'
          laying the basis for characterizing onto-
          logically the entities within-the-world as
          material Nature
p.132 273. The ontological problematics of a Thing-
          ontology and of value predicates
p.133 274. Descartes' Thing-ontology and later attempts
          to round it out
      275. The "passing over the world" and its being
          grounded in the mode of Dasein
      276. Critical questions concerning the Cartesian
          ontology of the world
p.134 277. Methodical considerations about the access
          to a positive understanding of the problem-
          atic of the world
      278. Criticism of the Cartesian ontology of the
          world as preparation for Heidegger's point
          of departure in his ontology of Dasein
      279. The significance of Descartes' idea of
          extensio

          C. THE AROUNDNESS OF THE ENVIRONMENT
          AND DASEIN'S SPATIALITY (pp.134-148)

p.134 280. Preliminary methodical considerations about
          the access to Dasein's spatiality and the
          way the world is spatially determined

          22. The Spatiality of the Ready-
          to-hand Within-the-world
              (pp.135-138)

p.135 281. Methodical considerations about the inter-
          connection of space, world, and the ready-
          to-hand
      282. The unfolding of the understanding of the
          characterization of the ready-to-hand and
          its relationship to the Being of what is
          within-space -- closeness, place, equipment
          belonging somewhere, region
p.136 283. Characterization of region as direction and
          range

S.103 284. Die vorgängige Zuhandenheit der jeweiligen
          Gegend
S.104 285. Umwelt, Welt und Dasein

23. Die Räumlichkeit des
In-der-Welt-seins (S.104-110)

S.104 286. Ent-fernung und Ausrichtung als Charaktere
          des Daseins hinsichtlich seines In-der-
          Welt-seins
S.105 287. Entfernung als Existenzial im Unterschied
          zu Entferntheit und Abstand als kategoria-
          len Bestimmungen
      288. Nähe als wesenhafte Tendenz des Daseins
      289. Entferntheit und Nähe des innerweltlich Zu-
          handenen und die objektiven Abstände vor-
          handener Dinge
S.106 290. Umsichtiges Ent-fernen der Alltäglichkeit
          des Daseins und Entdeckung des An-sich-
          seins der "wahren Welt"
      291. Das umsichtige Besorgen als das über Nähe
          und Ferne des umweltlich zunächst Zuhande-
          nen Entscheidende
S.107 292. In-der-Nähe-sein als ein in dem Umkreis des
          umsichtig zunächst Zuhandenen Sein
S.108 293. Die phänomenale Eigentümlichkeit der Ent-
          fernungsstruktur des In-seins -- Dasein als
          wesenhaft Ent-fernung-(dh räumlich-) sein
      294. Umsichtiges Besorgen als ausrichtendes
          Ent-fernen
      295. Rechts und links in Verbindung mit der Ver-
          räumlichung des Daseins in seiner "Leiblich-
          keit"
S.109 296. Die Fundierung der Ausrichtung durch das
          In-der-Welt-sein
      297. "Etwas im Gedächtnis haben" als existenzia-
          le Verfassung des In-der-Welt-seins
S.110 298. Zusammenfassung über Ent-fernung und Aus-
          richtung

24. Die Räumlichkeit des Daseins
und der Raum (S.110-113)

S.110 299. Bedeutsamkeit als Grund für die mit der
          Weltlichkeit der Welt wesenhafte Miter-
          schlossenheit des Raumes

40

p.137 284. The readiness-to-hand which belongs to any
          region beforehand
      285. Range, world, and Dasein

          23. The Spatiality of Being-in-
              the-world (pp.138-144)

p.138 286. De-severance and directionality of Dasein's
          characters with regard to its Being-in-the-
          world
p.139 287. The existentiale deseverance in distinction
          from the categories deservedness and dis-
          tance
      288. Closeness as essential tendency of Dasein
p.140 289. Remoteness and closeness of what is ready-
          to-hand within-the-world and the objective
          distance of things present-at-hand
p.141 290. The circumspective de-serving of Dasein's
          everydayness and revealing the Being-in-
          itself of the "true world"
      291. Circumspective concern as that which decides
          as to the closeness and farness of what is
          proximally ready-to-hand environmentally
p.142 292. "Being close by" as Being within the range
          of what is proximally ready-to-hand for
          circumspection
      293. The phenomenal peculary of the de-
          severance structure of Being-in -- Dasein
          as Being essentially de-serving (that is
          Being spatial)
p.143 294. Circumspective concern as de-serving which
          gives directionality
      295. "Right" and "left" in relation to Dasein's
          spatialization in its "body nature"
      296. The founding of directionality upon the
          Being-in-the-world
p.144 297. To have something "in the memory" as exis-
          tential constitutive state of Being-in-the-
          world
      298. Summary of de-severance and directionality

          24. Space and Dasein's Spatiality
                   (pp.145-148)

p.145 299. Significance as the basis for the disclosed-
          ness of space which is essentially co-
          disclosed with the worldhood of the world

S.110 300. Die vorgängige Entdecktheit des Raumes als
           die des Phänomens der Gegend -- als das Wo-
           hin der möglichen Zugehörigkeit des zuhan-
           denen Zeugzusammenhanges
S.111 301. Einräumen bzw. Raum-geben als Existenzial
           -- Freigeben des Zuhandenen auf seine Räum-
           lichkeit und als Ermöglichung der jeweili-
           gen faktischen Orientierung
      302. Die Apriorität des Raumes als Vorgängigkeit
           des Begegnens von Raum als Gegend im jewei-
           ligen umweltlichen Begegnen des Zuhandenen
      303. Die Räumlichkeit des Daseins und sein Raum
S.112 304. Der homogene Naturraum und die Welt
      305. Der Unterschied zwischen Martin Heidegger
           und Descartes bei der Interpretation des
           Seins des Raumes
S.113 306. Methodische Erwägungen zum Ansatz für das
           Verständnis des ontologischen Raumproblems
      307. Der Raum und die primäre ontologische Be-
           stimmtheit des Seins des innerweltlichen
           Seienden

Kapitel 4

DAS IN-DER-WELT-SEIN ALS MIT- UND
SELBSTSEIN. DAS "MAN" (S.113-130)

S.113 308. Methodische Erwägungen zum Aufbau dieses
           Kapitels

25. Der Ansatz der existenzialen Frage
    nach dem Wer des Daseins (S.114-117)

S.114 309. Das Wer des Daseins als Ich selbst -- Sub-
           jekt und Selbst
S.115 310. Die ontische Selbstverständlichkeit des Wer
           und die Problematik seiner ontologischen
           Interpretation
      311. Methodische Erwägungen:
           1. Über die Sicherung des Ansatzes der exi-
           stenzialen Frage nach dem Wer

p.145 300. "Space having been disclosed beforehand"
as disclosedness of the phenomenon of the
region -- the "whither" to which an equipment context ready-to-hand might possibly
belong
p.146 301. "Giving space" or "making room" as existentiale -- the freeing of the ready-to-hand
for its spatiality and the making possible
of one's factical orientation
302. The "apriority" of space as the previous-
ness with which space has been encountered
as region whenever the ready-to-hand is encountered environmentally
303. Dasein's spatiality and its space
p.147 304. The homogeneous space of Nature and the
world
305. The difference between Descartes and Martin
Heidegger concerning the Interpretation of
space
306. Methodical considerations about the point
of departure for the understanding of the
ontological problem of space
p.148 307. Space and the primary ontological character
of the Being of entities within-the-world

Chapter IV

BEING-IN-THE-WORLD AS BEING-WITH
AND BEING-ONE'S-SELF. THE "THEY"
(pp.149-168)

p.149 308. Methodical considerations about the organization of chapter IV

25. An Approach to the Existential
Question of the "who" of Dasein
(pp.150-153)

p.150 309. The "who" of Dasein as the "I" itself --
subject and self
310. The obvious ontical assertion about the
"who" and the problematic of its ontological Interpretation
p.151 311. Methodical considerations:
1. About the appropriate point of departure
concerning the existential question of
the "who"

43

S.115 312. 2. Über das Problem der Gegebenheit des Ich
als Zugang zu einer formalen Phänomeno-
logie des Bewusstseins
313. Ich als unverbindliche formale Anzeige ver-
schiedener Seinsarten des "Ich" selbst
S.116 314. Das Ich und das Schon-mit-da-sein der Anderen als im In-der-Welt-sein Gegebenes
315. Die mit der ontischen Selbstverständlichkeit des An-sich-sein des innerweltlich
Seienden und der der Jemeinigkeit des Daseins gegebene ontologische Problematik
S.117 316. Das "Ich" als essentielle Bestimmtheit des
Daseins und die Notwendigkeit seiner existenzialen Interpretation
317. Die "Substanz" des Menschen als Existenz

26. Das Mitdasein der Anderen und das alltägliche Mitsein (S.117-125)

S.117 318. Methodische Erwägungen zum Ansatz von Abschnitt 26
319. Der Unterschied der Seinsarten des innerweltlich begegnenden Daseins der Anderen
und des im innerweltlich begegnenden Seienden von nicht-daseinsmässigen Charakter
S.118 320. Das mithafte In-der-Welt-sein als die je
schon immer mit dem Anderen geteilte Welt
-- Mitwelt, Mitsein, Mitdasein als Strukturen des mithaften In-der-Welt-seins
S.119 321. Das Sich-selbst-finden des Daseins in dem
zunächst besorgten umweltlichen Zuhandenen
322. Die Notwendigkeit, das Ich-hier aus der
existenzialen Räumlichkeit des Daseins zu
verstehen
323. Hier, da und dort als Charaktere der ursprünglichen Räumlichkeit des Daseins, die
primär existenziale Bedeutung haben
S.120 324. Das Mitdasein-in-der-Welt des Anderen als
Zugang zur Begegnung des Anderen
325. Die möglichen Weisen des Mitseins
S.121 326. Fürsorge und Mitsein
327. Die Seinsmodi der Fürsorge als Seinsmodi
des Miteinanderseins
S.122 328. Die beiden extremen Möglichkeiten der positiven Modi der Fürsorge:
1. Das Einspringen für den Anderen

44

p.151 312. 2. About the problem of the givenness of
the "I" as access to a formal phenomenology of consciousness
313. The "I" as non-committal formal indicator
of various modes of the "I" itself
p.152 314. The "I" and Being-already-there-with-Others
as given in Being-in-the-world
315. The problematic given with the ontical ob-
viousness of Being-in-itself of entities
within-the-world and Dasein's mineness
316. The "I" as an essential characteristic of
Dasein and the necessity of its existential
Interpretation
p.153 317. The "substance" of the human person as
existence

      26. The Dasein-with of Others and
      Everyday Being-with (pp.153-163)

p.153 318. Methodical considerations about the point
of departure for section 26
319. The difference of modes between the Dasein
of Others encountered within-the-world and
entities with a character other than that
of Dasein encountered within-the-world
p.154 320. The with-like Being-in-the-world as the
world in which one always shares already
with Others -- with-world, Being-with,
Dasein-with as structures of the with-like
Being-in-the-world
p.155 321. Dasein's finding itself in the things environmentally ready-to-hand with which it is
proximally concerned
322. The necessity to understand the "I here" in
terms of Dasein's existential spatiality
p.155 323. "Here", "there", and "yonder" as characters
of Dasein's primordial spatiality which
have a primarily existential signification
p.156 324. The Dasein-with of the Others in the world
as access to encountering the Other
325. The possible ways of Being-with
p.157 326. Solicitude and Being-with
p.158 327. The modes of solicitude as modes of Being-
with-one-another
328. The two extreme possibilities of the positive modes of solicitude:
1. The "leaping in" for the Other

45

S.122 329. 2. Das dem Anderen Vorausspringen bezüglich
          seines existenziellen Seinkönnens
      330. Die beiden Möglichkeiten der Fürsorge --
          das Miteinandersein als Abstand und als
          eigentliche Verbundenheit
      331. Der "Standort" des alltäglichen Miteinan-
          derseins
S.123 332. Rücksicht und Nachsicht als das die Fürsor-
          ge Leitende
      333. Das eigene Sein des Daseins als das Sein,
          worumwillen das Dasein selbst ist, wie es
          ist
      334. Die Weltlichkeit der Welt und die existen-
          ziale Wesensaussage vom Mitsein als als dem
          wesenhaft umwillen Anderer seienden Dasein
      335. Der Charakter der zum Mitsein gehörenden
          Erschlossenheit des Mitdaseins Anderer als
          des Verständnisses Anderer
S.124 336. Notwendigkeit besonderer Wege zum Anderen
          als Ergebnis der sich in defizienten oder
          indifferenten Modi aufhaltenden Fürsorge
      337. "Einfühlung":
          1. Die Seinsart des Miteinanderseins als
          das Sichoffenbaren und Verschliessen
      338. 2. Die Annahme, dass das Sein mit und zu
          Anderen ein Seinsverhältnis von Dasein
          zu Dasein sei
      339. 3. Die Fragwürdigkeit der Voraussetzung des
          Anderen als einer Dublette des Selbst
S.125 340. 4. Mitsein als das die Einfühlung Ermög-
          lichende
      341. Ergebnis der Analyse von "Einfühlung", Mit-
          sein, Mitdasein und Miteinandersein
      342. Zusammenfassung von Abschnitt 26

          30. Das alltägliche Selbstsein
             und das Man   (S.126-130)

S.126 343. Die Analyse des Mitseins und ihr ontolo-
          gisch relevantes Ergebnis
      344. Das Miteinandersein und sein existenzialer
          Charakter der Abständigkeit
      345. Das Man als das alltägliche Miteinandersein
          unter der Herrschaft der Anderen

p.158 329. 2. The "leaping ahead" of the Other with
regard to his existentiell potentiality-
for-Being
p.159 330. The two possibilities of solicitude -- Being-
with-one-another as distance and as "Being
authentically bound together"
331. The "position" of everyday "Being-with-one-
another"
332. Considerateness and forbearance as that
which guides solicitude
p.160 333. Dasein's ownmost Being as Being "for the
sake of which" Dasein is itself as it is
334. The worldhood of the world and Being-with
as an existential statement to its essence
with regard to the Dasein which is essentially for the sake of Others
335. The character of Being-with to which belongs
the disclosedness of the Dasein-with Others
as understanding of Others
p.161 336. The necessity of special routes to come to
Others as result of solicitude which dwells
in deficient or indifferent modes
337. "Empathy":
1. The mode of Being-with-one-another as
"opening oneself up" and "closing oneself off"
p.162 338. 2. The assumption that Being-with and "Being
towards Others" be a relationship of
Being from Dasein to Dasein
339. 3. The dubiousness of the presupposition
concerning the Other as a duplicate of
the Self
340. 4. Being-with as that which makes "empathy"
possible
341. Results of the analysis of "empathy," Being-
with, Dasein-with, and Being-with-one-
another
342. Summary of section 26

27. Everyday Being-one's-Self and
the "They" (pp.163-168)

p.163 343. The analysis of Being-with and its ontologically relevant results
344. Being-with-one-another and its existential
character of distantiality
p.164 345. The "they" as the everyday Being-with-one-
another under the domination of the Others

47

S.126 346. Das Man als das die Seinsart der Alltäglich-
          keit Vorschreibende
S.127 347. Abständigkeit, Durchschnittlichkeit und
          Einebnung als Seinsweisen des Man
      348. Die "Öffentlichkeit" als Verfassung der dem
          Man zugehörigen Seinsweisen
      349. Flucht vor der Entscheidung als Kennzeich-
          nung des Man
      350. Seinsentlastung und Entgegenkommen als
          Seinscharaktere der Alltäglichkeit
S.128 351. Das Man als das Niemand
      352. Das Man als Seiendes in der Seinsweise der
          Unselbständigkeit und Uneigentlichkeit
      353. Das Problem der Zugängigkeit des Man
      354. Der Unterschied von Man und "allgemeinem
          Subjekt"
S.129 355. Das Man als Existenzial und die Verfassung
          des Daseins
      356. Die Interpretation des Mitseins und Selbst-
          seins im Man -- das Man-selbst
      357. Das formale Ergebnis der Frage nach dem Wer
          der Alltäglichkeit des Miteinanderseins
S.130 358. Die Verfehlung der ontologischen Interpre-
          tation der Seinsverfassung des In-der-Welt-
          seins und ihr Ursprung
      359. Eigentliches Selbstsein und existenzielle
          Modifikation des Man
      360. Die Selbigkeit des eigentlich existierenden
          Selbst und die Identität des Ich

Kapitel 5

DAS IN-SEIN ALS SOLCHES (S.130-180)

28. Die Aufgabe einer thematischen
Analyse des In-Seins (S.130-134)

S.130 361. Zusammenfassung über den bisherigen Weg der
          phänomenalen Charakteristik des In-der-
          Welt-seins
      362. Gründe für die Vorwegnahme des Strukturmo-
          mentes "In-der-Welt-sein" und für die Rück-
          lenkung auf das Phänomen des In-Seins

48

p.164 346. The "they" as that which prescribes the
          Being of everydayness
      347. Distantiality, averageness, and "levelling
          down" as ways of the Being of the "they"
p.165 348. Publicness as constitution of the modes
          which belong to the "they"
      349. Escaping decision as characteristic of the
          "they"
      350. Disburdening of Being and accomodating as
          the characters of Being of everydayness
      351. The "they" as the "nobody"
p.166 352. The "they" as an entity in the modes of the
          failure to stand by one's Self and of
          authenticity
      353. The problem of the accessibility of the
          "they"
      354. The difference between the "they" and a
          "universal subject"
p.167 355. The "they" as existentiale and the consti-
          tution of Dasein
      356. The interpretation of Being-with and of
          Being-one's-Self in the "they" -- the
          they-self
      357. The formal result of the question concerning
          the "who" of the everydayness of Being-with-
          one-another
p.168 358. The passing over of the ontological state of
          the Being of Being-in-the-world and its
          source
      359. The authentic Being-one's-Self and the
          existentiell modification of the "they"
      360. The selfsameness of the authentically
          existentiell Self and the identity of the
          "I"

Chapter V

BEING-IN AS SUCH
(pp.169-224)

28. The Task of a Thematic Analysis
    on Being-in (pp.169-172)

p.169 361. Summary of the previous way of character-
          izing the phenomenon of Being-in-the-world
      362. Reasons for the advance orientation of the
          structural item of Being-in-the-world and
          for turning back to the phenomenon of
          Being-in

S.131 363. Zum Problem der Gleichursprünglichkeit kon-
stitutiver Elemente in der Ontologie
S.132 364. Methodische Erwägungen zum Ansatz für das
In-Sein
365. Das "Da" als das Seiende, das wesenhaft
durch das In-der-Welt-sein konstituiert ist
S.133 366. Dasein und Erschlossenheit
367. Die notwendigen Charakteristiken der Konstitution des In-Seins
368. Die beiden Hauptthemen der Explikation des
Da-seins
369. Die konstitutiven Weisen des Seins des Da
370. Aufgliederung von Abschnitt A
371. Erwägungen über die Analyse der Seinscharak-
tere des Da-seins
372. Aufgliederung von Abschnitt B

A. DIE EXISTENZIALE KONSTITUTION DES DA
(S.134-166)

29. Das Da-sein als Befindlichkeit
(S.134-140)

S.134 373. Der ontische Aspekt der Befindlichkeit
374. Weisen des Gestimmtseins des Daseins
375. Die stimmungsmässige Erschlossenheit des
Seins des Da
S.135 376. Geworfenheit, Faktizität und Dasein
377. Befindlichkeit, Geworfenheit und Abkehr
378. Befindlichkeit als Existenzial und ihre Abgrenzung gegenüber Rationalismus und Irra-
tionalismus
S.136 379. Wesensbestimmung der Befindlichkeit:
1. Erschliessung der Geworfenheit:
a) Befindlichkeit als ausweichende Abkehr
380. b) Befindlichkeit und seelischer Zustand
381. 2. Jeweiliges Erschliessen des ganzen In-
der-Welt-seins
382. 3. Umsichtig besorgendes Begegnenlassen als
Betroffenwerden
S.137 383. 4. Zusammenfassung -- Weltoffenheit des Daseins und Gestimmtheit der Befindlich-
keit

50

p.169 363. The problem of the equiprimordiality of the
            constitutive items in ontology
p.170 364. Methodical considerations about the point
            of departure for the discussion of the
            Being-in
p.171 365. The "there" as that entity which is essen-
            tially constituted by Being-in-the-world
      366. Dasein and disclosedness
      367. The necessary characteristics of the
            constitution of Being-in
      368. The two main themes of the explication of
            Being-in
      369. The constitutive ways of the Being of the
            "there"
p.172 370. Organization of the themes of section A
      371. Considerations about the analysis of the
            characteristics of the Being of Being-there
      372. Arrangement of the themes of section B

      A. THE EXISTENTIAL CONSTITUTION
         OF THE "THERE" (pp.172-210)

      29. Being-there as State-of-mind
             (pp.172-179)

p.172 373. The ontical aspect of state-of-mind
p.173 374. Ways of Dasein's "having a mood"
      375. The moodwise disclosedness of the Being of
            the "there"
p.174 376. Thrownness, facticity, and Dasein
      377. State-of-mind, thrownness, and the turning-
            away
p.175 378. State-of-mind as existentiale and its
            demarcation concerning rationalism and
            irrationalism
      379. Determination of the nature of the state-of-
            mind:
            1. The disclosing of Dasein's thrownness
               a) State-of-mind as evasive turning-away
      380.   b) State-of-mind and psychical conditions
      381. 2. Current disclosing of Being-in-the-world
               as a whole
      382. 3. "Letting something be circumspectively
               encountered" as something that matters
               to us
p.176 383. 4. Summary -- Dasein's openness to the world
               and the attunement of the state-of-mind

51

S.138 384. Existenzial-ontologische Konstitution des
          erkennenden Bestimmens und Gefühl
      385. Die Interpretation der Affekte und Gefühle
          bei Aristoteles
S.139 386. Die Interpretation der Affekte und Gefühle
          in der Stoa, der patristischen und schola-
          stischen Theologie sowie in der Neuzeit
      387. Die Interpretation der Affekte und Gefühle
          bei Max Scheler
      388. Das Wesen der Befindlichkeit als existen-
          zialer Seinsart des Daseins
      389. Befindlichkeit als eine existenziale Grund-
          art
S.140 390. Gründe für das Thema in Abschnitt 30

          30. Die Furcht als ein Modus
          der Befindlichkeit (S.140-142)

S.140 391. Die drei Betrachtungsweisen der Furcht
      392. Das "Furchtbare" als das Wovor der Furcht
S.141 393. Das Fürchten selbst als Furchtsamkeit
      394. Das Worum der Furcht:
          1. Allgemeine Erwägungen
      395. 2. Fürchten um als Sichfürchten vor
      396. 3. Das Fürchten für als Sichfürchten
S.142 397. Die verschiedenen Seinsmöglichkeiten des
          Fürchtens

          31. Das Da-sein als Verstehen
             (S.142-148)

S.142 398. Verstehen als erschliessendes Seinkönnen
          des Da
S.143 399. Kennzeichnung des Verstehens in Verbindung
          mit dem In-der-Welt-sein
      400. Möglichkeit als Existenzial
S.144 401. Dasein als Möglichkeit des Freiseins für
          das eigene Seinkönnen
      402. Der Zusammenhang von Verstehen und Möglich-
          keit
      403. Die Struktur des Existenzials des Verstehens
      404. Das Verstehen und sein Dringen in die Mög-
          lichkeiten

p.177 384. The existential-ontological Constitution of cognitive determining and feeling
p.178 385. Aristotle's interpretation of affects and feelings
386. The interpretation of affects and feelings in Stoic philosophy, in patristic and scholastic theology, and in modern times
387. Max Scheler's interpretation of affects and feelings
388. The nature of the state-of-mind as an existential kind of Being of Dasein
389. State-of-mind as a basic existential way of Dasein
p.179 390. Reasons for the theme of section 30

30. Fear as a Mode of State-of-Mind (pp.179-182)

p.179 391. The three points of view for the consideration of fear
392. The "fearsome" as that in the face of which we fear
p.180 393. The fearing as such as "fearfulness"
394. That which fear fears about:
1. General considerations
p.181 395. 2. "Fearing about" as "being-afraid in the face of something"
396. 3. "Fearing for" as "being-afraid-for-oneself"
397. The different possibilities of Being with regard to fearing

31. Being-there as Understanding (pp.182-188)

p.182 398. Understanding as a disclosive potentiality-for-Being of the Being of the "there"
399. Characterization of understanding in connection with Being-in-the-world
p.183 400. Possibility as an existentiale
401. Dasein as the possibility of Being-free for its ownmost potentiality-for-Being
402. The interconnection of understanding and possibility
p.184 403. Proposition concerning the structure of the existentiale of understanding
404. Understanding and its pressing forward into possibilities

53

S.145 405. Der Entwurfcharakter des Verstehens
406. Die Konsequenzen des Entwurfcharakters des Verstehens
S.146 407. Die Seinsarten von Verstehen und von Dasein
408. Verstehen und faktisches Dasein
409. Sicht und Eigentlichkeit des Daseins:
1. Durchsichtigkeit des Daseins als Selbsterkenntnis
410. 2. Undurchsichtigkeit des Daseins
S.147 411. Sicht und Gelichtetheit
412. Verstehen als Existenzial und als Grund für Anschauung, Denken und phänomenologische Wesensschau
413. Vorweggenommenes Seinsverständnis und Entwerfen auf Möglichkeit
S.148 414. Zusammenfassung über das Da-sein als Verstehen und die damit gegebene Problematik
415. Hinweis auf die Notwendigkeit der Ausarbeitung der Existenzialien der alltäglichen Seinsart des befindlichen Verstehens

32. Verstehen und Auslegen (S.148-153)

S.148 416. Kennzeichnung der Auslegung
417. Wahrnehmen von zuhandenem Zeug als verstehendes Auslegen
S.149 418. Die spezifische Erschliessungsfunktion der Auslegung
S.150 419. Die Fundierung der alltäglich umsichtigen Auslegung durch die Bewandtnisganzheit -- Vorhabe, Vorsicht und Vorgriff
420. Auslegung und Vorverständnis
421. Die Problematik des Begreifens des Charakters des Vorverständnisses
S.151 422. Methodische Erwägungen zur Untersuchung des Vorverständnisses
423. Der Sinn als das im verstehenden Erschliessen Artikulierbare
S.152 424. Das Unsinnige
425. Die Frage nach dem Sinn von Sein
426. Auslegung, Zirkel und herkömmliches Verstehen der Geschichte

p.184 405. The character of understanding as projection
p.185 406. The consequences of the character of understanding as projection
p.186 407. The kinds of Being with regard to understanding and to Dasein
408. Understanding and factical Dasein
409. <u>Sight and the authenticity of Dasein:</u>
1. Transparency of Dasein as knowledge of
the Self
p.187 410. 2. Dasein's opaqueness
411. Sight and clearedness
412. Understanding as existentiale and as basis
for intuition, thinking, and phenomenological intuition of essences
413. The previously stated understanding of
Being and projecting upon possibilities
p.188 414. Summary of Being-there as understanding
and the problematics which emerge in this
context
415. The necessity of working out the existen-
tialia of the everyday kind of Being concerning an understanding with a state-of-
mind

32. <u>Understanding and Inter-
pretation</u> (pp. 188-195)

p.188 416. The characterization of interpretation
p.189 417. Perceiving of equipment that is ready-to-
hand as an interpreting that understands
p.190 418. The specific way in which interpretation
functions as disclosure
p.191 419. The founding of the everyday circumspective
interpretation by a totality of involvements -- fore-having, fore-sight, and
fore-conception
420. Interpretation and prior-understanding
p.192 421. The problematic of conceiving the character
of prior-understanding
422. Methodical considerations about the
explication of prior-understanding
423. Meaning as that which an understanding
interpretation Articulates
p.193 424. Unmeaning
425. The inquiry about the meaning of Being
p.194 426. Interpretation, the circle and the traditional understanding of history

S.153 427. Die Notwendigkeit des Zirkels für das Verstehen
428. Der Zirkel des Verstehens als Konstituens
der Struktur des Sinnes

33. Die Aussage als abkünftiger
Modus der Auslegung (S.153-160)

S.153 429. Auslegung und Aussage
S.154 430. Methodische Erwägungen zur Analyse der Aussage
431. Die drei Bedeutungen der Aussage:
432. 1. Aussage als Aufzeigung
433. 2. Aussage als Prädikation
S.155 434. 3. Aussage als Mitteilung
435. Die Fragwürdigkeit einer an der Geltung
orientierten Urteilstheorie
S.156 436. Definition und Kennzeichnung der Aussage
S.157 437. Der ursprüngliche Vollzug der Auslegung
illustriert an einem Beispiel
438. Die Nivellierung des ursprünglichen "Als"
der umsichtigen Auslegung zum "Als" der Vor-
handenweitsbestimmung
S.158 439. Die beiden extremen Weisen der Auslegung
440. Der Zwischenbereich von Auslegungen
441. Die Struktur des Logos und das Phänomen des
apophantischen "Als":
S.159 442. 1. Die formale Struktur des Logos bei Plato
und Aristoteles
443. 2. Das Phänomen des "etwas als etwas" bei
Aristoteles
444. 3. Beziehen und Urteil
445. 4. Die Copula und der Zusammenhang des Problems der existenzialen Analytik
S.160 446. Die Verwurzelung des Logos in der existenzialen Analytik des Daseins und die Nicht-
ursprünglichkeit der methodischen Basis der
antiken Ontologie

34. Da-sein und Rede. Die Sprache
(S.160-166)

S.160 447. Zusammenfassung der Abschnitte 30-33 und
Einführung in Abschnitt 34

p.194 427. Understanding and the necessity of the circle

428. The circle in understanding as constituting element of the structure of meaning

33. Assertion as a Derivative Mode of Interpretation (pp.195-203)

p.195 429. Interpretation and assertion

p.196 430. Methodical considerations about the analysis of assertions

431. The three significations of the term "assertions":

432. 1. Assertion as "pointing out"

433. 2. Assertion as "prediction"

p.197 434. 3. Assertion as "communication"

p.198 435. The dubiousness of a theory of judgment which is oriented to validity

p.199 436. Definition and characterization of assertion

p.200 437. The primordial carrying out of interpretation

438. The levelling of the primordial "as" of circumspective interpretation to the "as" with which presence-at-hand is given a definite character

p.201 439. The two extreme ways of interpretation

440. The realm between interpretations

441. The structure of the Logos and the apophantical "as":

442. 1. The formal structure of the Logos as found in Plato and Aristotle

p.202 443. 2. Aristotle's idea of the phenomenon of "something as something"

444. 3. Relating and judgment

445. 4. The copula and the interconnection of the problems of an existential analytic

p.203 446. Logos as rooted in the existential analytic of Dasein and the fact that the methodological basis of ancient ontology was not a primordial one

34. Being-there and Discourse. Language (pp.203-210)

p.203 447. Summary of sections 30-33 and introduction to section 34

57

S.161 448. Befindlichkeit, Verstehen und Rede
      449. Die Sprache als die Hinausgesprochenheit
           der Rede
      450. Hören und Schweigen
      451. Die Charaktere der Struktur der Rede als
           Reden über:
           1. Das Geredete
S.162 452. 2. Die Mitteilung
      453. 3. Das Sichaussprechen
      454. Das Kennzeichnende der Rede und ihrer Struk-
           turmomente
S.163 455. Die verschiedenen bisherigen Versuche, das
           Wesen der Sprache zu fassen
      456. Hören als existenzial primäres Hörenkönnen
      457. Horchen als verstehendes Hören
S.164 458. Hören und innerweltlich Zuhandenes
      459. Ausdrückliches Hören der Rede des Anderen
      460. Hören auf die Diktion als der Weise des
           Gesagtseins
      461. Gegenrede als Antwort
      462. Verstehen als der Grund von Reden und Hören
      463. Schweigen als wesenhafte Möglichkeit des
           Redens
S.165 464. Der Mensch als das Seiende, das Rede hat
S.166 465. Das Problem der Seinsart der Sprache
      466. Zusammenfassung über die Absicht von Ab-
           schnitt 34

      B. DAS ALLTÄGLICHE SEIN DES DA UND
DAS VERFALLEN DES DASEINS (S.166-180)

S.166 467. Methodische Erwägungen über:
           1. Die existenzialen Strukturen der Er-
              schlossenheit des In-der-Welt-seins als
              alltäglicher Seinsart des Man
S.167 468. 2. Die mögliche Erschliessbarkeit des Seins
              des Daseins als Man
      469. 3. Die alltägliche Seinsart von Rede, Sicht
              und Auslegung

p.203 448. State-of-mind, understanding, and discourse
p.204 449. Language as way in which discourse gets expressed
      450. Hearing and keeping silent
      451. The character of the structure of discourse as discourse about:
           1. The something said-in-the-talk as such
p.205 452. 2. Communication
      453. 3. The expressing itself
p.206 454. The characteristics of discourse and its structural items
      455. The various attempts to grasp the essence of language
      456. Hearing as existentially primary potentiality for hearing
p.207 457. Hearkening as hearing which understands
      458. Hearing as the ready-to-hand within-the-world
      459. The explicite hearing of the discourse of Others
      460. Hearing the diction as the way in which something is said
      461. Counter-discourse as answer
      462. Understanding as the basis of talking and hearing
p.208 463. Keeping silent as an essential possibility of discourse
      464. The human person as the entity that has discourse
p.209 465. The problem of the kind of Being of language
p.210 466. Summary about the intention of the discussion in section 34

      B. THE EVERYDAY BEING OF THE "THERE,"
      AND THE FALLING OF DASEIN (pp.210-224)

p.210 467. Methodical considerations:
           1. About the existential structures of the disclosedness of Being-in-the-world so far as the latter is an everyday kind of Being of the "they"
      468. 2. About the possible disclosedness of Dasein's Being as the "they"
      469. 3. About the everyday kind of Being of discourse, sight, and interpretation

59

35. Das Gerede (S.167-170)

S.167 470. Das Gerede als Phänomen, das die Seinsart des Verstehens und Auslegens des alltäglichen Seins konstituiert
S.168 471. Die Seinstendenzen der Mitteilung
472. Gerede und durchschnittliche Verständlichkeit
473. Das Sich-Konstituieren des Geredes in dem Weiterreden und Nachreden
S.169 474. Die Bodenlosigkeit des Geredes und der Eingang des Geredes in die Öffentlichkeit
475. Das Gerede als ein Verschliessen
476. Verschliessen als vermeintliches Verstehen seitens des Geredes
477. Die Herrschaft der alltäglichen öffentlichen Ausgelegtheit
S.170 478. Das Gerede als Seinsart des entwurzelten Daseinsverständnisses
479. Die Folgen der Seinsmöglichkeit der Entwurzelung des Daseinsverständnisses

36. Die Neugier (S.170-173)

S.170 480. Lichtung des Daseins und Sicht
481. Neugier als eigentümliche Seinstendenz der Alltäglichkeit zum "Sehen":
1. Sehen und Wissenschaft bei Aristoteles und Parmenides
S.171 482. 2. Der merkwürdige Vorrang des Sehens bei Augustinus
S.172 483. Einleitende Fragen über die Tendenz zum Nur-Vernehmen
484. Neugier als Sorge des Sehens, dh als Aufenthaltslosigkeit
485. Unverweilen, Zerstreuung und Aufenthaltslosigkeit als die Wesenscharaktere der Neugier
S.173 486. Gerede und Neugier als alltägliche Seinsmodi von Rede und Sicht

37. Die Zweideutigkeit (S.173-175)

S.173 487. Der Umkreis der Zweideutigkeit
488. Die Kennzeichnung der Zweideutigkeit als Auf-der-Spur-sein

60

35. Idle Talk
(pp.211-214)

p.211 470. Idle talk as phenomenon which constitutes
the kind of Being of everyday Dasein's
understanding and interpreting
471. Communication and its tendency of Being
p.212 472. Idle talk and average intelligibility
473. Idle talk as being constituted by gossiping
and passing the word along
p.213 474. The groundlessness of idle talk and its
becoming public
475. Idle talk as closing off
476. Closing off as a supposed understanding
reaching in idle talk
477. The dominance of the public way of everydayness in which interpretation has taken
place
p.214 478. Idle talk as the kind of Being which belongs
to the uprooted understanding of Dasein
479. The consequences of the possibility-of-Being
of the uprooted understanding of Dasein

36. Curiosity
(pp.214-217)

p.214 480. Clearing of Dasein and sight
481. Curiosity as the peculiar tendency-of-Being
of everydayness towards seeing:
1. Aristotle's and Parmenides' ideas about
seeing and science
p.215 482. 2. The remarkable priority of seeing noticed
by Augustine
p.216 483. Introductory question about the tendency
just to perceive
484. Curiosity as care of seeing, i.e., as "never
dwelling anywhere"
485. Not-tarrying, distraction, and never-
dwelling-anywhere as essential characteristics of curiosity
p.217 486. Idle talk and curiosity as everyday modes
of Being for discourse and sight

37. Ambiguity
(pp.217-219)

p.217 487. The extension of ambiguity
488. The characterization of ambiguity as Being-
on-the-scent

61

S.173 489. Gerede und Wirklichkeit
S.174 490. Gerede und Zweideutigkeit sowie das Hervor-
           treten des neu und echt Geschaffenen
      491. Das Verstehen des Daseins im Man und die
           Zweideutigkeit des Daseins
      492. Die Funktion der Zweideutigkeit bei Neugier
           und Gerede
      493. Die Zweideutigkeit des Miteinanderseins im
           Man als Gegeneinandersein
S.175 494. Die Zweideutigkeit als Vorhandenes in dem
           geworfenen Miteinandersein in einer Welt
      495. Methodische Erwägungen bezüglich der Abhand-
           lung über Gerede, Neugier und Zweideutigkeit

      <u>38. Das Verfallen und die Geworfenheit</u>
                    (S.175-180)

S.175 496. Gerede, Neugier und Zweideutigkeit als Ent-
           hüllungen des Verfallens des Daseins
      497. Die Verfallenheit an die Welt als Uneigent-
           lichkeit des Daseins
S.176 498. Verfallen und der Fall aus einem Urstand
      499. Das Verfallen als existenziale Bestimmung
           des Daseins selbst
      500. Die Wertfreiheit der existenzial-ontologi-
           schen Struktur des Verfallens
      501. Das Phänomen des Verfallens als Dokumenta-
           tion eines existenzialen Modus des In-der-
           Welt-seins
S.177 502. Ontologische Verdeutlichung der Seinsart des
           alltäglichen In-der-Welt-seins an Gerede,
           Neugier und Zweideutigkeit
      503. Methodische Erwägungen über die "Bewegtheit"
           des Verfallens
      504. Die im Dasein sich ständig bereitende Ver-
           suchung zum Verfallen
      505. Das verfallende In-der-Welt-sein als ver-
           meintliche Beruhigung des Daseins, dh als
           Beruhigung im uneigentlichen Sein
      506. Die Beruhigung im uneigentlichen Sein als
           Ursache für die Hemmungslosigkeit des Be-
           triebs und als Entfremdung
S.178 507. Entfremdung als Verschliessung der Eigent-
           lichkeit und Möglichkeit des Daseins --
           das Sichverfangen des Daseins

p.218 489. Idle talk and that which actually happens
      490. Idle talk and ambiguity as well as the
           emergence of that which is newly and
           genuinely created
      491. Dasein's understanding in the "they" and
           Dasein's ambiguity
p.219 492. The function of ambiguity in relation to
           curiosity and idle talk
      493. The ambiguity of Being-with-one-another as
           Being-against-one-another
      494. Ambiguity as something present-at-hand in
           the thrown Being-with-one-another in a world
      495. Methodical considerations with regard to the
           discussion about idle talk, curiosity, and
           ambiguity

           38. Falling and Thrownness
              (pp.219-224)

p.219 496. Idle talk, curiosity, and ambiguity as
           revealing Dasein's falling
p.220 497. Fallenness into the world as Dasein's
           inauthenticity
      498. Falling and the fall from a primal status
      499. Falling as existential characteristic of
           Dasein itself
      500. The ontologico-existential structure of
           falling as one that is free from values
p.221 501. The phenomenon of falling as documentation
           of an existential mode of Being-in-the-
           world
      502. Elucidating ontologically the kind of Being
           that belongs to everyday Being-in-the-world
           as it shows through idle talk, curiosity,
           and ambiguity
      503. Methodical considerations about the move-
           ment of falling
      504. The constant temptation towards falling
           which Dasein prepares for itself
p.222 505. Falling Being-in-the-world as supposed
           tranquility of Dasein -- as tranquility
           in inauthentic Being
      506. The tranquility in inauthentic Being as
           source of the uninhibited hustle and as
           alienation
      507. Alienation as closing off of authenticity
           and as Dasein's possibility -- Dasein's
           getting entangled

63

S.178 508. Der Absturz als Seinsart des Verfallens und
der sie kennzeichnenden Phänomene
509. Der Wirbel als Bewegtheit des Verfallens
und als immer Vortäuschen und doch Losreis-
sen von der Eigentlichkeit
S.179 510. Das Kennzeichnende der Geworfenheit
511. Das Verfallen und die Existenzialität des
Daseins
512. Das Verfallen als wesenhaft ontologische
Struktur des Daseins selbst
513. Der Zusammenhang von Glaube und Weltanschau-
ung mit der existenzialen Struktur
S.180 514. Zusammenfassung über das In-Sein als solches
515. Martin Heideggers Anliegen in Kapitel 1-5

Kapitel 6

DIE SORGE ALS SEIN DES DASEINS
(S.180-230)

39. Die Frage nach der ursprünglichen Ganzheit des Strukturganzen des Daseins
(S.180-184)

S.180 516. Das In-der-Welt-sein als ursprüngliche,
ständig ganze Struktur und die phänomenale
Vielfalt der Verfassung dieses Strukturganzen
S.181 517. Das Selbst und die Bestimmung der durch-
schnittlichen Alltäglichkeit des Daseins
518. Methodische Erwägungen zur Erfassung des
Strukturganzen der Alltäglichkeit:
519. 1. Negative Abgrenzung einer möglichen Erfassung des Strukturganzen der Alltäglichkeit
S.182 520. 2. Verstehende Befindlichkeit im Dasein als
Problem eines Weges zur Erfassung des
Strukturganzen der Alltäglichkeit
521. 3. Die Notwendigkeit eines Weges zur Erschliessung des Daseins, in der das Dasein sich vor sich selbst bringt
522. 4. Angst und Sorge
523. 5. Erwägungen zur existenzialen Interpretation des Daseins als Sorge
S.183 524. 6. Erwägungen zum Begriff von Realität
525. 7. Erwägungen zum Phänomen der Wahrheit

p.223 508. The downward plunge as kind of Being of
           falling and of the phenomena that charac-
           terize that specific kind of Being
      509. Turbulence as movement of falling and as
           constantly tearing away of authenticity
           though always with a sham of authenticity
      510. The characteristic of thrownness
      511. Falling and Dasein's existentiality
p.224 512. Falling as an essential ontological struc-
           ture of Dasein itself
      513. The interconnectedness of belief and world-
           view with the existential structures
      514. Summary of Being-in as such
      515. Martin Heidegger's concern in chapters 1-5

Chapter VI

CARE AS THE BEING OF DASEIN (pp.225-273)

39. The Question of the Primordial
Totality of Dasein's Structural Whole
(pp.225-228)

p.225 516. Being-in-the-world as a structure which
           is primordially and constantly whole and
           the phenomenal manifoldness of the consti-
           tution of this structural whole
      517. The Self and the definition of Dasein's
           average everydayness
p.226 518. Methodical considerations about grasping
           the structural whole of everydayness:
      519. 1. The negative demarcation of a possible
              grasping of the structural whole of
              everydayness
      520. 2. The understanding state-of-mind in Da-
              sein as the problem of a way leading to
              the structural whole of everydayness
      521. 3. The necessity of a way to disclose Da-
              sein, in which Dasein brings itself be-
              fore itself
p.227 522. 4. Anxiety and care
      523. 5. Considerations about Dasein's existen-
              tial interpretation of care
      524. 6. Considerations about the conception of
              reality
p.228 525. 7. Considerations about the phenomenon of
              truth

65

S.184 526. Die Themen von Kapitel 6

40. Die Grundbefindlichkeit der Angst als eine ausgezeichnete Erschlossenheit des Daseins (S.184-191)

S.184 527. Angst, Befindlichkeit und das Problem ihres Zusammenhangs

528. Methodische Erwägungen über Angst als ausgezeichnete Befindlichkeit des Daseins: 1. Die Flucht des Daseins vor ihm selbst und seiner Eigentlichkeit als Ausgangspunkt für eine Bestimmung der Angst

529. 2. Gründe für die Möglichkeit des existenzial-ontologischen Fassens des Wovor der Flucht

S.185 530. 3. Die Interpretation des Verfallenseins als Explikation dessen, was das Dasein selbst ontisch erschliesst

531. 4. Die phänomenale Verwandtschaft zwischen Furcht und Angst

532. Furcht und die Abkehr des Verfallens: 1. Das Wovor der Angst:

S.186 533. a) Die Abkehr des Verfallens und ihre Gründung in der Angst

534. b) Das Wovor der Angst als das In-der-Welt-sein und die Unbestimmtheit dieses Wovor

535. c) Das bedrohende Nirgends als das Kennzeichnende des Wovor der Angst

536. d) Angst und die Unbedeutsamkeit des Innerweltlichen

S.187 537. e) Die Welt als die Möglichkeit des Zuhandenen überhaupt und als Nichts

538. f) Die Erschliessung der Welt als Welt und die Angst als Modus der Befindlichkeit

539. 2. Das Worum der Angst: a) Das In-der-Welt-sein selbst und das Erschliessen des Daseins als Möglichkeit

S.188 540. b) Die Angst und die Möglichkeit des "Freiseins für"

p.228 526. The main themes of chapter VI

40. The Basic State-of-mind
of Anxiety as a Distinctive
Way in which Dasein is Disclosed (pp.228-235)

p.228 527. Anxiety, state-of-mind, and the problem of
their interconnection
p.229 528. Methodical considerations about anxiety as
a distinctive state-of-mind of Dasein:
1. Dasein's fleeing in the face of itself
and in the face of its authenticity as
point of departure for determining
anxiety
529. 2. Reasons for the possibility of grasping
existential-ontologically that in the
face of which Dasein flees
530. 3. The interpretation of Dasein's falling
as explication of what Dasein itself
ontically discloses
p.230 531. 4. Fear and anxiety as kindred phenomena
532. Fear and the turning-away of falling:
1. That in the face of which one has
anxiety:
533. a) The turning-away of falling and its
being grounded in anxiety
534. b) That in the face of which one has
anxiety as Being-in-the-world and
the indeterminacy of that in the
face of which one has anxiety
p.231 535. c) The threatening "nowhere" as that
which characterizes that in the face
of which one has anxiety
536. d) Anxiety and the insignificance of
what is within-the-world
537. e) The world as the possibility of the
ready-to-hand in general and as
nothing
p.232 538. f) The disclosure of the world as world
and anxiety as a mode of the state-
of-mind
539. 2. The "about" of anxiety:
a) Being-in-the-world itself and its
disclosing of Dasein as possibility
540. b) Anxiety and the possibility of Being-
free-for

S.188 541. Vereinzelung und Erschliessung des Daseins
als alleinstehendes und verlassenes Selbst
durch die Angst
542. Angst als Offenbarung der Unheimlichkeit --
als das In-der-Welt-sein im Sinne des Unzu-
hauseseins
S.189 543. Die Unheimlichkeit als Bedrohung der alltäglichen Verlorenheit des Daseins in das Man
544. Die Angst als Grundbefindlichkeit des Daseins und die Unheimlichkeit
545. Furcht als defizienter Modus der Angst
S.190 546. Die physiologische Auslösung der Angst
547. Die faktische Seltenheit des Phänomens der
Angst
548. Gründe für die ausgezeichnete Stellung der
Angst
S.191 549. Methodisch vorbereitende Frage zur Sorge

41. Das Sein des Daseins als Sorge
(S.191-196)

S.191 550. Die fundamentalen ontologischen Charaktere
der Angst als ursprünglicher Zusammenhang
der Ganzheit des Strukturganzen des Daseins
551. "Freisein für" und die Struktur des Sich-
vorweg-seins des Daseins
S.192 552. Die Struktur des Sich-vorweg-im-schon-sein-
in-einer-Welt
553. Das Sich-vorweg-im-schon-sein-in-einer-Welt
und das wesenhafte Verfallensein des Daseins
554. Die formal existenziale Ganzheit des ontologischen Strukturganzen des Daseins und die
ontologisch-existenzial aufgefasste Sorge
S.193 555. Die kennzeichnenden Strukturmomente der
Sorge
556. Das Sich-vorweg-sein als Bedingung der Möglichkeit des "Freiseins für" und die Uneigentlichkeit des Daseins
557. Die als ursprüngliche Strukturganzheit exi-
stenzial-apriorisch gegebene Sorge
558. Die Unmöglichkeit, das Phänomen der Sorge
auf bestimmte Akte und Triebe zu reduzieren
S.194 559. Die Verwurzelung von Wollen, Wünschen, Hang
und Drang in der Sorge
560. Die Einheit des Phänomens der Sorge
561. Das Phänomen des Wollens
562. Das beruhigte "Wollen" unter der Führung
des Man
S.195 563. Das Phänomen des Wünschens
564. Das Phänomen des Hanges

p.233 541. Anxiety in its individualization and disclosing of Dasein as the Self which stands
alone and lost
542. Anxiety as revealing uncanniness -- Being-
in-the-world as Being-not-at-home
543. Uncanniness as threat of Dasein's everyday
lostness in the "they"
p.234 544. Anxiety as Dasein's basic state-of-mind and
uncanniness
545. Fear as a deficient mode of anxiety
546. Anxiety as conditioned by physiological
factors
547. The factical rarity of anxiety as a phenomenon
p.235 548. Reasons for the distinct position of anxiety
549. Preparatory methodical question concerning
care

41. Dasein's Being as Care
(pp.235-241)

p.235 550. The fundamental ontological characters of
anxiety as the primordial interconnection
of Dasein's totality of its structural whole
p.236 551. Being-free-for and Dasein's structure of
Being-ahead-of-itself
552. The structure of ahead-of-itself-in-already-
being-in-a-world
553. The ahead-of-itself-in-already-being-in-a-
world and Dasein's essential falling
p.237 554. The formally existential totality of
Dasein's structural whole and the
ontologico-existential grasping of care
555. The characteristic structural items of care
556. Being-ahead-of-oneself as condition for the
possibility of Being-free-for and Dasein's
inauthenticity
p.238 557. Care as primordial structural whole which is
given existentially and a priori
558. The impossibility to trace the phenomenon
of care back to special acts or drives
559. Willing, wishing, urge, and addiction as
rooted in care
560. The unity of the phenomenon of care
561. The phenomenon of willing
p.239 562. Tranquillized willing under the guidance of
the "they"
563. The phenomenon of wishing
p.240 564. The phenomenon of addiction

S.195 565. Das Phänomen des Dranges
S.196 566. Die Sorge als "Grund" von Hang und Drang
      567. Methodische Erwägungen über die Sorge als
           existenzial-ontologisches Grundphänomen

42. Die Bewährung der existenzialen Interpretation des Daseins als Sorge aus der vorontologischen Selbstauslegung
(S.196-200)

S.196 568. Methodische Erwägungen:
           1. Über die angemessenen ontologischen Fun-
              damente des Menschseins
S.197 569. 2. Über das sich vorontologisch aussprechen-
              de Seinsverständnis, das im Dasein
              selbst liegt
      570. Lateinischer Text der Cura-Fabel des Hyginus
S.198 571. Text der Übersetzung der Cura-Fabel von
           K. Burdach
      572. Die Cura-Fabel als Zeugnis für das Primäre
           der Sorge als Wissen um die Zeitlichkeit
S.199 573. Der Doppelsinn von "cura" als ängstliche
           Bemühung und als Sorgfalt und Hingabe
      574. Die Grundverfassung der Sorge
      575. Der Unterschied von theoretisch-ontischer
           und existenzial-ontologischer Interpreta-
           tion der Sorge
      576. Die transzendentale "Allgemeinheit" des
           Phänomens der Sorge und die ontisch-welt-
           anschauliche Daseinsauslegung
S.200 577. Die ontisch sich aufdrängende "Allgemein-
           heit" und ihre ontologische Bestimmtheit
      578. Methodische Erwägungen zur bisherigen onto-
           logischen Interpretation des Daseins

43. Dasein, Weltlichkeit und Realität
(S.200-212)

S.200 579. Das Seinsverständnis und die Seinsart des
           Daseins
      580. Zusammenfassung über das bisherige Ergebnis
           der vorbereitenden existenzialen Analytik
           des Daseins
S.201 581. Die existenziale Analytik des Daseins und
           die Realität als Substanzialität

p.240 565. The phenomenon of urge
      566. Care as ground of addiction and urge
      567. Methical considerations about care as a
           basic existential-ontological phenomenon

           42. Confirmation of the Existential
           Interpretation of Dasein as Care
           in terms of Dasein's Pre-ontological
           Way of Interpreting Itself
                (pp.241-244)

p.241 568. Methical considerations:
           1. About the appropriate ontological foun-
              dation of Being human
      569. 2. About that understanding of Dasein which
              lies in Dasein itself and which expresses
              itself pre-ontologically
p.242 570. Latin text of the Cura Fable of Hyginus
      571. Translation of Hyginus' Cura Fable
p.243 572. The Cura Fable as a document for care point-
           ing to care as being primary and as knowl-
           edge of temporality
      573. The double meaning of the term "cura" as
           anxious exertion but also carefulness and
           as devotedness
      574. The basic constitution of care
      575. The difference between theoretical-ontical
           and existential-ontological interpretation
           of care
p.244 576. The transcendental generality of the phe-
           nomenon of care and Dasein's ontical inter-
           pretation by means of a world-view
      577. The generality which obtrudes itself
           ontically and its ontological definiteness
      578. Methical considerations about the previous
           ontological interpretation of Dasein

           43. Dasein, Worldhood, and
           Reality (pp.244-256)

p.244 579. Understanding of Being and Dasein's kind
           of Being
      580. Summary of the results achieved by the
           previous pursuit of the preparatory exis-
           tential analytic of Dasein
p.245 581. Existential analytic of Dasein and reality
           as substantiality

S.201 582. Methodische Erwägungen zur Untersuchung des Seins im Sinne von Realität:
        1. Grundsätzliches
      583. 2. Das Realitätsproblem

      (a) Realität als Problem des Seins und die Beweisbarkeit der "Aussenwelt" (S.202-208)

S.202 584. Bewusstsein als bisheriger Ausgangspunkt für das Erkennen des Realen und die damit verbundenen Probleme
      585. Erkennen in der existenzialen Analytik und seine Fundierung in der Grundverfassung des Daseins als In-der-Welt-sein
      586. Die Idee der Realität der Aussenwelt als fragwürdiger und verwirrender Ausgangspunkt für die Ontologie
S.203 587. Imanuel Kants Position:
        1. Der fragwürdige und verwirrende Ansatz bei Kant
      588. 2. Dasein als Vorhandenheit bei Kant
      589. 3. Kants Beweis für das "Dasein der Dinge ausser mir"
S.204 590. 4. Kants Versuch des Beweises für ein notwendiges Zusammenvorhandensein von wechselndem und beharrlichem Seienden in Verbindung mit der Position von Descartes
      591. Die von Kant übernommene Position von Descartes und das grundsätzlich damit verbundene Problem
      592. Martin Heideggers Kritik an der Position von Kant
S.205 593. Die Unmöglichkeit des Nachweises einer Aussenwelt
      594. Die Fragwürdigkeit des Glaubens an eine Aussenwelt als Ausgangsposition für die Realität der Aussenwelt
S.206 595. Der Vorrang des "Apriori" der Seinsverfassung in der Seinsart der Sorge als das allem Erkennen Vorausgehende
      596. Die Voraussetzung eines weltlosen Subjektes als fragwürdige Ausgangsposition für das Problem der Realität einer Aussenwelt

p.245 582. Methodical considerations about the analysis
of Being in the sense reality:
1. Basic aspects
583. 2. The problem of reality

(a) Reality as a problem of Being,
and whether the "External World"
can be proved (pp.246-252)

p.246 584. Consciousness as the customary point of departure for the knowing of reality and the
problems which are related to it
585. The idea of knowing in existential analytic
and its being founded in Dasein's basic
constitution as Being-in-the-world
586. The idea of the reality of the "external
world" as a dubious and confusing point of
departure for ontology
p.247 587. The position held by Imanuel Kant:
1. The dubious and confusing point of departure exhibited by Kant
588. 2. Kant's idea of Dasein as presence-at-
hand
589. 3. Kant's proof for the "Dasein of Things
outside of me"
p.248 590. 4. Kant's attempted proof for entities that
are changing and such that are permanent
and which are necessarily present-at-
hand together, a proof which he carried
out by basing it on Descartes' position
591. Kant's adopting of Descartes' position and
the basic problem connected with this
position
592. Martin Heidegger's criticism of Kant's
position
p.249 593. The impossibility of demonstrating an
external world
594. The dubiousness of a belief in an external
world as the position of a departure for
investigating the reality of an external
world
595. The priority of the a priori of the constitution of Being in the kind of Being of care
as that which precedes all knowledge
p.250 596. The presupposition of a worldless subject
as a dubious position of the departure for
investigating the problem of the reality of
an external world

73

S.206 597. Die Unmöglichkeit der "Realität" im Sinne
           der Frage des Vorhandenseins und der Be-
           weisbarkeit einer Aussenwelt
       598. Die unangemessene Fragestellung aller bis-
           herigen erkenntnistheoretischen Richtungen
           in der Philosophie
S.207 599. Die existenziale Aussage des Vorhandenseins
           von innerweltlich Seiendem:
           1. Und der Realismus
       600. 2. Und der Idealismus
S.208 601. 3. Und die beiden möglichen Bedeutungen des
           Idealismus
       602. Die Realitätsproblematik vor jeder "stand-
           punktlichen" Orientierung und die existen-
           ziale Aussage des Vorhandenseins von inner-
           weltlich Seiendem
       603. Ergebnis der Untersuchungen über Realität
           als Problem des Seins

   (b) Realität als ontologisches Problem
       (S.209-211)

S.209 604. Absteckung der Fundamente und Horizonte,
           durch deren Klärung die Analyse von Reali-
           tät ermöglicht wird
       605. Wilhelm Diltheys Kennzeichnung der Realität
           als Widerständigkeit und die damit gegebe-
           nen Probleme
S.210 606. Max Schelers voluntative Daseinstheorie als
           Aufnahme der Realitätsinterpretation von
           Wilhelm Dilthey
       607. Erschliessung von Welt als Voraussetzung
           der Widerständigkeit
S.211 608. Realitätsbewusstsein als Weise des In-der-
           Welt-seins
       609. Martin Heideggers neue Interpretation des
           cogito sum und der damit verbundene Neuan-
           satz des Realitätsproblems

   (c) Realität und Sorge   (S.211-212)

S.211 610. Zurückweisung des üblicherweise postulier-
           ten Vorranges der Realität
       611. Der Zusammenhang von Realität und Sorge

p.250 597. The impossibility of reality in the sense of presence-at-hand and of proving an external world

598. The inappropriate formulation of the question in the different epistemologies and the epistemological directions of philosophy

p.251 599. The existential assertion of the Being of presence-at-hand of entities within-the-world:
1. And realism

600. 2. And idealism

601. 3. And the two possible meanings asserted in idealism

602. The problematics of reality prior to every orientation in terms of standpoints and the existential assertion of the Being of presence-at-hand of entities within-the-world

603. Results of the analysis of reality as a problem of Being

(b) Reality as an Ontological Problem (pp.252-254)

p.252 604. Demarcation of the foundations and horizons which must be clarified if an analysis of reality is to be possible

605. Wilhelm Dilthey's characterization of reality as resistance and the problems connected with this idea

p.253 606. Max Scheler's voluntative theory of Dasein as one that takes up Wilhelm Dilthey's interpretation of reality

607. Disclosure of the world as presupposition for the character of resisting

p.254 608. Consciousness of reality as a way of Being-in-the-world

609. Martin Heidegger's new interpretation of the "cogito sum" and the new point of departure for the problem of reality which is connected with his interpretation

(c) Reality and Care (pp.254-256)

p.254 610. Rejection of the traditionally postulated priority of reality

p.255 611. The interconnection between reality and care

75

S.212 612. Die Abhängigkeit des Seins vom Seinsver-
         ständnis des Daseins
      613. Die Existenzialität und die Abhängigkeit
         der Realität von der Sorge
      614. Die Existenz als die "Substanz" des Men-
         schen und die damit verbundenen Probleme
         der existenzialen Analytik

      44. Dasein, Erschlossenheit und Wahrheit
                    (S.212-230)

S.212 615. Wahrheit und Sein in der griechischen Philo-
         sophie bei Parmenides und Aristoteles
S.213 616. Der antike Wahrheitsbegriff und die damit
         verbundenen Probleme
      617. Erwägungen über einen möglichen Zusammen-
         hang von Wahrheit und Dasein
      618. Methodische Erwägungen über die Stelle der
         Wahrheit in der existenzialen Analytik
S.214 619. Aufbau und Gliederung von Abschnitt 44

      (a) Der traditionelle Wahrheitsbegriff und seine
          ontologischen Fundamente (S.214-219)

S.214 620. Die drei Thesen der traditionellen Auffas-
         sung des Wesens der Wahrheit
      621. Methodische Erwägungen über die Entfaltung
         des Abschnittes 44a
      622. Aristoteles Wahrheitsbegriff und seine Auf-
         nahme in der mittelalterlichen Philosophie
S.215 623. Der Wahrheitsbegriff in der neukantischen
         Erkenntnislehre des 19. Jahrhunderts
      624. Der Wahrheitsbegriff bei Kant in seiner
         "Kritik der reinen Vernunft"
      625. Untersuchung über Wahrheit als Übereinstim-
         mung:
      626. 1. Das die Übereinstimmung Kennzeichnende
S.216 627. 2. Erkenntnis als Urteilen und die damit
         verbundenen Probleme
      628. 3. Bestand als ontologisches Problem
      629. 4. Das Problem des ontologischen Sinnes der
         methexis als Beziehung zwischen Realem
         und Idealem
S.217 630. 5. Das Problem der Einheit von realem Voll-
         zug und idealem Gehalt
      631. Erwägungen über die Seinsart des Erkennens:
      632. 1. Wahrnehmung, Aussage und wahres Erkennen

76

p.255 612. The dependence of Being on Dasein's understanding of Being
613. Existentiality and reality's dependence on care
614. Existence as man's "substance" and the problems of existential analytic

44. Dasein, Disclosedness, and Truth (pp.256-273)

p.256 615. Parmenides' and Aristotle's association of truth and Being
616. The conception of truth in ancient Greek philosophy and the problem which it created
617. Considerations about a possible interconnection between truth and Dasein
618. Methodical considerations about the locus of truth within existential analytic
p.257 619. Arrangement of the main themes of section 44

(a) The Traditional Conception of Truth, and its Ontological Foundations (pp.257-261)

p.257 620. The three theses which characterize the way in which the essence of truth has been traditionally understood
621. Methodical considerations about the unfolding of the discussion in section 44a.
622. Aristotle's conception of truth and its acceptance in medieval philosophy
p.258 623. The neo-Kantian epistemology and its conception of truth
624. Kant's conception of truth found in his Critique of Pure Reason
625. Analysis of truth as agreement:
626. 1. That which characterizes agreement
p.259 627. 2. Knowledge as judging and the problem connected with this assumption
628. 3. Subsisting as ontological problem
629. 4. The problem of the ontological meaning of methexis as relation between real and ideal
630. 5. The problem of the unity of the real act of judgment and the ideal content of judgment
p.260 631. Considerations about the kind of Being that belongs to knowledge:
632. 1. Perceiving, assertion, and genuine knowing

S.218 633. 2. Entdeckend-sein als Struktur des Wahr-
seins
S.219 634. 3. Entdeckend-sein und In-der-Welt-sein

(b) Das ursprüngliche Phänomen der Wahrheit und
die Abkünftigkeit des traditionellen Wahrheitsbegriffes (S.219-226)

S.219 635. Wahrheit bei den Griechen als Unverborgen-
heit verstanden
S.220 636. Verhinderung der Nivellierung der Kraft ele-
mentarer Worte als Aufgabe des Philosophen
637. Die phänomenale Ausweisung des über Logos
und Aletheia Gesagten durch die Definition
der Wahrheit
638. Der Ausgangspunkt der Definition der Wahrheit
639. Der Zugang zu dem ursprünglichen Phänomen
der Wahrheit
640. Wahrheit als Entdeckend-sein [Entdeckung]
und als Entdecktsein [Entdecktheit]
641. Die Erschlossenheit des Daseins als In-der-
Wahrheit-sein des Daseins
S.221 642. Der Satz "Dasein ist in der Wahrheit":
643. 1. Die Seinsverfassung des Daseins und die
Erschlossenheit überhaupt
644. 2. Die Seinsverfassung des Daseins und die
Geworfenheit
645. 3. Die Seinsverfassung des Daseins und der
Entwurf -- Wahrheit der Existenz als ursprünglichste und eigentlichste Erschlossenheit
646. 4. Die Seinsverfassung des Daseins und das
Verfallen
S.222 647. Dasein, Schein und Entdecktheit
648. Die faktische Entdecktheit als Raub aus der
Verborgenheit
649. Dasein als in der Wahrheit und in der Unwahrheit seiend
S.223 650. Die existenzial-ontologische Bedingung für
die Gleichursprünglichkeit des Seins in der
Wahrheit und in der Unwahrheit
651. Ergebnis der existenzial-ontologischen Interpretation des Phänomens des Daseins
652. Methodische Erwägungen über die traditionelle Interpretation des Wahrheitsphänomens
653. Die Herkunft der Aussagewahrheit aus der
Erschlossenheit des Daseins

p.261 633. 2. Being-uncovering as structure of Being-
true
634. 3. Being-uncovering and Being-in-the-world

(b) The Primordial Phenomenon of Truth
   and the Derivative Character of the
   Traditional Conception of Truth
       (pp.262-269)

p.262 635. The Greek's understanding of Being-true as
Being-uncovering
636. The task of philosophy as one of preventing
that the force of the most elemental words
is levelled off
637. The phenomenological demonstration of what
has been set forth as to Logos and Aletheia
by defining truth
p.263 638. The point of departure for defining truth
639. The access to the primordial phenomenon of
truth
640. Being-true as Being-uncovering (uncovering)
and as Being-uncovered (uncoveredness)
641. Dasein's disclosedness as its Being-in-the-
world
642. The proposition "Dasein is in the truth":
p.264 643. 1. Dasein's constitution of Being and disclosedness in general
644. 2. Dasein's constitution of Being and
thrownness
645. 3. Dasein's constitution of Being and projection -- truth of existence as most
primordial and authentic disclosedness
646. 4. Dasein's constitution of Being and falling
p.265 647. Dasein, semblance, and uncoveredness
648. Factical uncoveredness as robbery by
snatching entities out of their hiddenness
649. Dasein being in truth as well as in untruth
650. The existential-ontological condition of
Dasein's equiprimordially Being in truth
and in untruth
651. The result of the existential-ontological
interpretation of the phenomenon of truth
652. Methodical considerations about the traditional interpretation of the phenomenon of
truth
p.266 653. The truth of assertions originating in
Dasein's disclosedness

S.223 654. Wahrheit als Übereinstimmung von Aussage und Urteil und die ontologische Abkünftigkeit dieses traditionellen Wahrheitsbegriffes:
1. Aussage, Rede und Erschlossenheit des Daseins
S.224 655. 2. Die Aussage als Zuhandenes
S.225 656. Zusammenfassung über die "Wahrheit" als Übereinstimmung von der Erkenntnis mit ihrem Gegenstand
657. Das Ergebnis der Zueignung der Entdecktheit durch Hörensagen des Gesagten als einer Seinsart des Man
658. Die Verdeckung des Phänomens der Wahrheit durch das zunächst herrschende Selbstverständnis
659. Wahrheit und Seinsverständnis in der griechischen Philosophie
S.226 660. Wahrheit und Seinsverständnis bei Aristoteles
661. Die Fragwürdigkeit der These von dem Urteil als dem genuinen Ort der Wahrheit
662. Wahrheit als Existenzial

(c) Die Seinsart der Wahrheit und die Wahrheitsvoraussetzung (S.226-230)

S.226 663. Das Dasein als Grund für die Wahrheit
S.227 664. Illustrierung dieses Zusammenhanges an den Gesetzen Newtons
665. Das Problem der ewigen Wahrheiten
666. Das Wesen der existenzial begriffenen Seinsart der Wahrheit
667. Der Sinn der Wahrheitsvoraussetzung
S.228 668. Das Wesen des Voraussetzens
669. Die Notwendigkeit des Voraussetzens von Wahrheit und der Skeptizismus
S.229 670. Wahrheit und Skepsis
671. Die Fragwürdigkeit des Ansetzens eines "idealen Subjektes"
672. Die Zurückweisung eines "Bewusstseins überhaupt"
673. Reste christlicher Theologie innerhalb der Philosophie
S.230 674. Die Gleichursprünglichkeit von Sein und Wahrheit
675. Die Möglichkeit echter Ontologie

p.266 654. Truth as agreement between assertion and judgment and the ontologically derivative character of the traditional conception of truth:
    1. Assertion, discourse, and Dasein's disclosedness
655. 2. The assertion "as something ready-to-hand"
p.267 656. Summary of truth as agreement between knowing and its object
657. The result of the appropriation of uncoveredness as a kind of Being of the "they" that is occasioned by passing on the word
p.268 658. The covering up of the phenomenon of truth by that understanding of Being which proximally prevails
659. Truth and understanding of Being in ancient Greek philosophy
660. Aristotle's idea of truth and his understanding of Being
p.269 661. The dubiousness of the theses that the genuine locus of the truth lies in the judgment
662. Truth as existentiale

(c) The Kind of Being which Truth Possesses, and the Presupposition of Truth (pp.269-273)

p.269 663. Dasein as the ground for truth
664. Illustration of the interconnectedness between Dasein and truth by using Newton's laws
665. The problem of "eternal truths"
p.270 666. The nature of the existential conceptions of the kind of Being that belongs to truth
667. The meaning of "presupposing the truth"
668. The nature of presupposing
p.271 669. The necessity of presupposing truth and scepticism
670. Truth and scepticism
p.272 671. The dubiousness of positing an "ideal subject"
672. Rejection of the conception of a "consciousness in general"
673. Residues of Christian theology within philosophical thought
674. Truth and the equiprimordiality of Being
675. The possibility of genuine ontology

2. Abschnitt:

DASEIN UND ZEITLICHKEIT

(S.231-437)

45. Das Ergebnis der vorbereitenden Fundamentalanalyse des Daseins und die Aufgabe einer ursprünglichen existenzialen Interpretation dieses Seienden (S.231-235)

S.231 678. Zusammenfassendes Ergebnis der Fundamentalanalyse des Daseins

679. Die Möglichkeit einer radikalen Ausarbeitung der Frage nach dem Sinn des Seins als
der Grundfrage aller Ontologie

680. Die mit der ontologischen Grundlage verbundenen Kriterien:

681. 1. Die in phänomenaler Anmessung gesicherte
hermeneutische Situation

S.232 682. 2. Vor-sicht und die Einheit der Seins-
strukturen

683. Methodische Erwägungen über die ursprüngliche ontologische Interpretation des Daseins:

684. 1. Handelt die bisherige Fundamentalanalyse
von der Existenzialität der Existenz?

S.233 685. 2. Welches ist die Vorhabe der hermeneutischen Situation bei der bisherigen Fundamentalanalyse?

686. 3. Ergebnis -- Das Problematische der bisherigen existenzialen Analyse des Daseins

687. Die Aufgabe der existenzialen Erhellung des
Seins des Daseins in seiner möglichen
Eigentlichkeit und Ganzheit:
1. Die Aufweisung eines eigentlichen Ganzseinkönnens des Daseins

S.234 688. 2. Das eigentliche Ganzseinkönnen des Daseins als Verfassung des ursprünglichen
Seins des Daseins

Division 2

DASEIN AND TEMPORALITY

(pp.274-488)

45. The Outcome of the Preparatory
Fundamental Analysis of Dasein,
and the Task of a Primordial
Existential Interpretation of
this Entity (pp.274-278)

p.274 678. The results of the fundamental analysis of
Dasein in Division 1
679. The possibility of radically working out the
question about the meaning of Being as the
basic question of all ontology
680. The problem of the criteria which are to be
used in connection with the ontological
foundation:
p.275 681. 1. The hermeneutical situation as one which
has been made secure in conformity with
the phenomena
682. 2. Fore-sight and the unity of the structures of Being
683. Methodical considerations about the primordial ontological interpretation of Dasein:
684. 1. Does the preceding fundamental analysis
concern itself with the existentiality
of existence?
p.276 685. 2. What is the fore-having of the hermeneutical situation in the preceding
fundamental analysis?
686. 3. Results -- the problematics of the existential analysis of Dasein carried out
thus far
687. The task of existentially bringing to light
Dasein's Being in its possibilities of
authenticity and totality:
1. Pointing out that Dasein has an authentic
potentiality-for-Being-a-whole
p.277 688. 2. Dasein's authentic potentiality-for-
Being-a-whole as the constitution of
Dasein's primordial Being

85

S.234 689. 3. Zeitlichkeit und Existenzialität des
              Daseins
S.235 690. 4. Die Zeitlichkeit und der traditionelle
              Zeitbegriff
      691. 5. Seinsverständnis und Zeit als Innerzei-
              tigkeit
      692. Aufbau des 2. Hauptabschnittes

                    Kapitel 1

        DAS MÖGLICHE GANZSEIN DES DASEINS
        UND DAS SEIN ZUM TODE (S.235-267)

        46. Die scheinbare Unmöglichkeit einer
        ontologischen Erfassung und Bestimmung
             des daseinsmässigen Ganzseins
                    (S.235-237)

S.235 693. Methodische Erwägungen über die Untersu-
              chung des möglichen Ganzseins des Daseins
S.236 694. Die ständige Unabgeschlossenheit des Da-
              seins als ein Wesensmoment der Grundverfas-
              sung des Daseins
      695. Die Erreichung der Gänze des Daseins als
              Verlust seines In-der-Welt-seins schlecht-
              hin
      696. Der Grund für die Unmöglichkeit, Dasein als
              seiendes Ganzes in seiner Ganzheit ontolo-
              gisch zu bestimmen
      697. Probleme bezüglich der Untersuchung der on-
              tologischen Seinsganzheit des Daseins
S.237 698. Der Aufbau von Kapitel 1

        47. Die Erfahrbarkeit des Todes der
        Anderen und die Erfassungsmöglichkeit
          eines ganzen Daseins   (S.237-241)

S.237 699. Der Tod als Erfahrung des Überganges zum
              Nichtmehrdasein
S.238 700. Methodische Erwägungen bezüglich des Ansat-
              zes über den Tod der Anderen:
      701. 1. Interpretation des Umschlages aus dem
              Dasein zum Nur-noch-vorhandensein

                         86

p.277 689. 3. Temporality and the existentiality of
Dasein
p.278 690. 4. Temporality and the traditional concept
of time
691. 5. The understanding of Being and within-
time-ness
692. The arrangement of the main themes of
division 2

Chapter I

DASEIN'S POSSIBILITY OF BEING-A-WHOLE,
AND BEING-TOWARDS-DEATH (pp.279-311)

46. The Seeming Impossibility of Getting
Dasein's Being-a-whole into Our Grasp
Ontologically and Determining Its
Character (pp.279-281)

p.279 693. Methodical considerations about the analysis of Dasein's Being-a-whole
694. "Having constantly something to be settled"
as one item of the basic constitution of
Dasein
p.280 695. Dasein's reaching its wholeness as utter
loss of its Being-in-the-world
696. The reasons for the impossibility of determining Dasein's character ontologically in
its Being-a-whole
697. Problems concerning the analysis of Dasein's ontological totality-of-Being
698. The main themes of chapter 1

47. The Possibility of Experiencing
the Death of Others, and the Possibility
of Getting a Whole Dasein into our Grasp
(pp.281-285)

p.281 699. The death of Others as experience of the
transition to no-longer-Dasein
700. Methodical considerations about the death
of Others as point of departure for the
analysis that is to be undertaken:
701. 1. Interpretation of the change-over from
Dasein's kind of Being to Being-just-
present-at-hand-and-no-more

S.238 702. 2. Das Unlebendige als Nur-noch-vorhandenes
des Daseins

703. 3. Ergebnis

704. Das Sterben Anderer als Ersatzthema für die
ontologische Analyse der Daseinsabgeschlos-
senheit und Ganzheit und das Problematische
dieses Ersatzthemas:
1. Der Verstorbene als Gegenstand des "Besorgens"

705. 2. Das Mitsein mit dem Toten und das faktische Nicht-mehr-dasein des Verstorbenen

706. 3. Der Tod des Verstorbenen als Erfahrung
eines Verlustes bei den Verbleibenden

S.239 707. 4. Der am Anderen erfahrene Tod als mögliches Thema für die Analyse von Daseins-
ende und Ganzheit

708. 5. Die Unmöglichkeit der Ersetzbarkeit des
eigenen Daseins durch anderes Dasein

709. 6. Vertretbarkeit eines Daseins durch ein
anderes Dasein als Seinsmöglichkeit des
Miteinanderseins in der Welt

S.240 710. 7. Die Unmöglichkeit einer Vertretung bei
der Seinsmöglichkeit, die das Zu-Ende-
kommen als Gänze des Daseins [dh den Tod]
ausmacht

711. 8. Ergebnis -- Die Unmöglichkeit, das Ganzsein des Daseins phänomenal zugänglich
zu machen

712. Methodische Erwägungen über den Ansatz zur
Untersuchung der Erfassungsmöglichkeit des
Todes:
1. Der Tod als existenziales Phänomen

713. 2. Sterben und Verenden als Übergang vom
Dasein zum Nichtmehrdasein

S.241 714. Methodische Anweisungen für die weiteren Untersuchungen in Kapitel 1

48. Ausstand, Ende und Ganzheit
(S.241-246)

S.241 715. Methodische Erwägungen:
1. Gründe für die notwendige Vorläufigkeit
der hier vorgelegten Untersuchung über
die ontologische Charakteristik von Ende
und Ganzheit

716. 2. Der Ansatz für die Kennzeichnung der existenzialen Begriffe von Ende und Ganzheit

88

p.281 702. 2. That which is unalive as Dasein's just-
            present-at-hand-and-no-more
p.282 703. 3. Result of these considerations
      704. The dying of Others as a substitute theme
            for the ontological analysis of Dasein's
            totality and the settling of its account
            and the problematics of this substitute
            theme:
            1. The deceased as an object of concern
      705. 2. Being-with the dead and the factical
            no-longer-Dasein of the deceased
      706. 3. The death of the deceased as a loss
            experienced by those who remain
      707. 4. Death as experienced in Others as a
            possible theme for our analysis of
            Dasein's end and totality
p.283 708. 5. The impossibility of substituting one's
            own Dasein by another Dasein
      709. 6. Dasein's ability to be represented by
            another Dasein as possibility of Being
            in Being-with-one-another in the world
p.284 710. 7. The impossibility of a substitution in
            relation to that possibility-of-Being
            which makes up Dasein's coming to an
            end and as wholeness
      711. 8. Result -- the impossibility to make
            Dasein's Being-a-whole accessible in a
            way that is appropriate to the phenomena
      712. Methodical considerations about the point
            of departure for the analysis of the onto-
            logical possibility of getting death into
            our grasp:
            1. Death as an existential phenomenon
      713. 2. Dying and perishing as transition from
            Dasein to no-longer-Dasein
p.285 714. Methodical hints for the subsequent
            analysis of chapter 1

            48. That which is Still Outstanding;
                the End; Totality (pp.285-290)

p.285 715. Methodical considerations:
            1. Reasons why this investigation of the
            ontological characterization of the end
            and totality is necessarily provisional
      716. 2. The point of departure for the charac-
            terization of the existential concepts
            of the end and totality

S.242 717. 3. Der Ausgangspunkt für die Erarbeitung des existenzialen Sinnes des Zu-Ende-kommens des Daseins

718. Drei Thesen über den Tod als Zusammenfassung des bisher über den Tod Erörterten

719. Ausstand als Kennzeichen der ständigen mit dem Tode endenden Unganzheit des Daseins und das zum Modus des Zusammen zugehörige Unzusammen:
1. Charakterisierung des Ausstandes

S.243 720. 2. Das Noch-nicht als dem Dasein zugehöriges Element

721. Das Noch-nicht des Daseins als Werden

722. Das Reifen der Frucht als Beispiel für einen Vergleich mit einem Seienden, zu dessen Seinsart das Werden gehört

S.244 723. Bisheriges Ergebnis der Untersuchung und weitere methodische Erwägungen zum Noch-nicht des Daseins

724. Reifen und Tod als ein Enden

725. In welchem Sinne muss der Tod als Enden des Daseins begriffen werden?

726. 1. Die verschiedenen Modi des Endens:
a) Enden als Aufhören und Fertigwerden

S.245 727. b) Vollendung als Modus der Fertigkeit

728. c) Enden als Verschwinden

729. 2. Die Modi des Endens und die Charakterisierung des Todes

730. 3. Das mit dem Tode gemeinte Enden als Sein zum Tode

731. Weitere methodische Erwägungen:
1. Die Notwendigkeit der ontologischen Aufklärung des Todes aus der Seinsart des Daseins

732. 2. Erwägungen zu den Phänomenen des Noch-nicht-seins, des Endens und der Ganzheit

S.246 733. 3. Die Sorge und die existenzialanalytische Interpretation des Todes

49. Die Abgrenzung der existenzialen Analyse des Todes gegenüber möglichen anderen Interpretationen des Phänomens
(S.246-249)

S.246 734. Methodische Erwägungen zur Abgrenzung der existenzialen Analyse des Todes

p.286 717. 3. The point of departure for working out
the existential meaning of Dasein's
coming-to-its-end
718. Three theses summarizing that which thus far
has been investigated about death
719. Outstanding as a constant "lack of totality"
which finds an end with death and the lack-
of-togetherness which belongs to the mode
of togetherness:
1. Characterization of the "outstanding"
p.287 720. a/b 2. The not-yet as an item which belongs
to existing Dasein
721. Dasein's not-yet as becoming
722. The ripening of fruit as example of a comparison with an entity to whose kind of
Being becoming belongs
p.288 723. Summary of the investigation undertaken thus
far and further methodical considerations
about Dasein's not-yet
724. Ripening and death as ending
p.289 725. In which sense must death be conceived as
the ending of Dasein?
726. 1. The various modes of ending:
a) Ending as stopping and getting fin-
ished
727. b) Fulfilling as mode of finishedness
728. c) Ending as disappearing
729. 2. The modes of ending and the characterization of death
730. 3. The ending which we have in view when we
speak of death as Being-towards-the-end
731. Further methodical considerations:
1. The necessity for ontologically clarifying death in terms of Dasein's kind of
Being
p.290 732. 2. Considerations about the phenomena of
Being-not-yet, ending, and totality
733. 3. The phenomenon of care and the interpretation of death by way of existential
analysis

49. How the Existential Analysis
of Death is Distinguished from
Other Possible Interpretations
of this Phenomenon (pp.290-293)

p.290 734. Methodical considerations about demarcating
the existential analysis of death

S.246 735. Die biologisch-ontische Erforschung des
           Todes
      736. Verenden, Ableben, Sterben
S.247 737. Die biographisch-historischen und die ethno-
           logisch-psychologischen Interpretationen
           des Todes
      738. Die diesseitige ontologische Interpretation
           des Todes und die ontisch jenseitige Speku-
           lation
S.248 739. Die Metaphysik des Todes
      740. Methodische Erwägungen:
           1. Über die Vorordnung der existenzialen
              Analyse bezüglich der Frage einer Biolo-
              gie, Psychologie, Theodizee und Theologie
              des Todes
      741. 2. Über die Notwendigkeit einer vorgängigen
              ontologischen Kennzeichnung der Seinsart
              des Hereinbrechens des Endes in die
              durchschnittliche Alltäglichkeit des Da-
              seins

        50. Die Vorzeichnung der existenzial-
          ontologischen Struktur des Todes
                   (S.249-252)

S.249 742. Zusammenfassung über den Tod als Sein zum
           Ende und die fundamentalen Charaktere des
           Seins des Daseins
S.250 743. Methodischer Ansatz zum Abschnitt 50
      744. Der Tod als Bevorstand:
           1. Der Tod ist nicht Ausstand
      745. 2. Abgrenzung des Todes gegen Vorhandenes,
              Zuhandenes und Mit-daseiendes
      746. 3. Abgrenzung des Todes gegen Seinsmöglich-
              keiten, die im Mitsein mit Anderen grün-
              den
      747. 4. Der Tod als ausgezeichneter Bevorstand
S.251 748. Angst als Grundbefindlichkeit des Daseins
           und der Tod
      749. Das Sein zum Tode als ursprünglich und we-
           senhaft dem Sein des Daseins zugehörig
S.252 750. Methodische Erwägungen über Sorge, Alltäg-
           lichkeit und Sein zum Tode

p.290 735. The biological-ontical exploration of death
p.291 736. Perishing, demise, and dying
      737. The biographical-historiological and the
           enthnological-psychological investigations
           of death
p.292 738. The this-worldly ontological interpretation
           of death and the ontical other-worldly
           speculation
      739. The metaphysic of death
      740. Methodical considerations:
           1. About the existential analysis and its
              superordination to the questions of a
              biology, psychology, theodicy, or
              theology of death
      741. 2. About the necessity to give beforehand
              an ontological characterization of the
              kind of Being in which the end enters
              into Dasein's average everydayness

           50. Preliminary Sketch of the
           Existential-ontological
           Structure of Death
              (pp.293-296)

p.293 742. Summary about death as Being-towards-the-
           end and the fundamental characteristics of
           Dasein's Being
      743. Methodical considerations about the dis-
           cussion in section 50
      744. Death as something impending:
           1. Death is not something still outstanding
p.294 745. 2. Demarcation of death from the present-at-
              hand, the ready-to-hand or the being-
              there-with-us
      746. 3. Demarcation of death from possibilities-
              of-Being which are based upon Being with
              Others
      747. a/b 4. Death as something distinctively
                  impending
p.295 748. Death and anxiety as Dasein's basic state-
           of-mind
      749. Being-towards-death as primordially and
           essentially belonging to Dasein's Being
p.296 750. Methodical considerations about care and
           everydayness

51. Das Sein zum Tode und die Alltäglichkeit des Daseins (S.252-255)

S.252 751. Methodische Erwägungen über das Verhältnis von dem Man und dem Dasein als dem Sein zum Tode

752. Der Tod als die Unauffälligkeit des Todesfalles beim Man

S.253 753. Das verdeckende Ausweichen vor dem Tode als ein die Alltäglichkeit beherrschendes Moment und als Versuchung

754. Das Man in seiner Besorgung einer ständigen Beruhigung über den Tod

S.254 755. Die Verweigerung des Mutes zur Angst vor dem Tode seitens des Man als Entfremdung des Daseins vor seinem eigensten, unbezüglichen Seinkönnen

756. Die verfallende Flucht vor dem Tode als Bezeugung des Seins zum Tode seitens der Alltäglichkeit des Daseins

S.255 757. Methodische Erwägungen über die Sicherung des vollen existenzialen Begriffes des Seins zum Tode

52. Das alltägliche Sein zum Ende und der volle existenziale Begriff des Todes (S.255-260)

S.255 758. Zusammenfassung über die bisherigen Ausführungen des Seins zum Ende

759. Die Zweideutigkeit des verdeckenden Ausweichens vor dem Tode im Man

S.256 760. Das Problem der Gewissheit des Todes:

761. 1. Gewissheit und Wahrheit

762. 2. Überzeugung als Modus der Gewissheit

763. 3. Gewiss-sein gegenüber dem Tod als Daseinsgewissheit

764. 4. Gewissheit beim Man als unangemessenes Fürwahrhalten

S.257 765. 5. Der Tod als sogenannte unleugbare "Erfahrungstatsache" in der Seinsweise des Man

766. 6. Die bloss empirische aber nicht apodiktische Gewissheit des Todes in der Seinsweise des Man

767. Die Kenntnis der Gewissheit des Todes seitens des Man und sein Ausweichen vor dieser Gewissheit

<u>51. Being-towards-death and</u>
<u>the Everydayness of Dasein</u>
(pp.296-299)

p.296 751. Methodical considerations about the comportment of the "they" and Dasein as Being-towards-death
    752. Death understood by the "they" as the inconspicuousness of a case of death
p.297 753. The evasive concealment in the face of death as an item which dominates everydayness and as temptation
   (754.) The "they" in its providing of constant tranquillization about death
p.298 755. The refusal of the "they" to permit us to have the courage for anxiety in the face of death as Dasein's alienation from its ownmost non-relational potentiality-for-Being
    756. Falling and fleeing in the face of death as attestation of Being-towards-death by Dasein's everydayness
p.299 757. Methodical considerations about securing a full existential conception of Being-towards-the-end

<u>52. Everyday Being-towards-the-end,</u>
<u>and the Full Existential Concep-</u>
<u>tion of Death</u> (pp.299-304)

p.299 758. Summary of the preceding discussion about Being-towards-the-end
    759. The "they" and its ambiguous manner of the evasive concealment in the face of death
p.300 760. <u>The problem of the certainty of death:</u>
    761. 1. Certainty and truth
    762. 2. Conviction as mode of certainty
    763. 3. Being-certain with regard to death as a distinctive certainty of Dasein
p.301 764. 4. The certainty which belongs to the mode of the "they" as an inappropriate way of holding-for-true
    765. 5. The mode of the "they" understanding death as a so-called undeniable fact of experience
    766. 6. The mode of the "they" and its certainty which is only empirical but not apodictic
    767. The knowledge of the certainty of death by the "they" and its evasion of this certainty

S.258 768. Das Verschieben der Möglichkeit des Todes
als die Verdeckung des Todes seitens des Man
769. Das Man und der Tod
770. Definition des vollen existenzial-ontologischen Begriffes des Todes
S.259 771. Das Problem des möglichen Ganzseins des Seienden, das wir selbst sind
772. Dasein und die Seinsart der Uneigentlichkeit
773. Methodische Erwägungen:
1. Über eigentliches Verstehen des Daseins
S.260 774. 2. Über die existenzielle Möglichkeit des
Daseins als eigentlichem Sein zum Tode

53. Existenzialer Entwurf eines
eigentlichen Seins zum Tode (S.260-267)

S.260 775. Methodische Erwägungen:
1. Bezüglich der Probleme und Ansätze über
die ontologische Möglichkeit eines
eigentlichen Seins zum Tode
776. 2. Über bisher erzielte methodische Ergeb-
nisse und ihre Konsequenzen
777. 3. Über die Unausweichlichkeit des eigentlichen Seins zum Tode
S.261 778. Das Sein zum Tode als Sein zu einer Möglichkeit des Daseins:
1. Das Sein zum Tode als besorgendes Aus-
sein auf seine Verwirklichung
779. 2. Gründe dafür, warum das Sein zum Tode
nicht den Charakter des besorgenden Aus-
seins auf seine Verwirklichung haben kann
780. 3. Die Bedeutsamkeit der Möglichkeit für das
Verstehen des Seins zum Tode
781. 4. Das Erwarten als Problem des Verhaltens
des Daseins zu Möglichem in seiner Möglichkeit
S.262 782. 5. Das Sein zum Tode als Vorlaufen in die
Möglichkeit und als Möglichkeit der Unmöglichkeit der Existenz überhaupt
783. Das Vorlaufen in den Tod als eigenste äus-
serste Möglichkeit eigentlicher Existenz:
S.263 784. 1. Der Tod als eigenste Möglichkeit des Daseins
785. 2. Die Unbezüglichkeit des Todes als eigenste Möglichkeit des Daseins

p.302 768. The deferring of the possibility of death
            by the "they" as its covering up of death
       769. The "they" and death
       770. Definition of the full existential-
            ontological conception of death
p.303 771. The problem of the possible Being-a-whole
            of that entity which each of us is
       772. Dasein, the kind of Being of inauthenticity,
            and death
p.304 773. Methodical considerations:
            1. About Dasein's authentic understanding of
            death
       774. 2. About Dasein's existentiell possibility
            as authentic Being-towards-death

       53. Existential Projection of
       an Authentic Being-towards-
       death (pp.304-311)

p.304 775. Methodical considerations:
            1. About the problems of the ontological
            possibility of authentic Being-towards-
            death
       776. 2. About the methodical results and conse-
            quences of the attempted investigation
       777. 3. About the inevitability of authentic
            Being-towards-death
p.305 778. Being-towards-death as Being towards a
       distant possibility of Dasein:
            1. Being-towards-death as a Being-out for
            that which is concerned with its actu-
            alization
       779. 2. Reasons why Being-towards-death cannot
            have the character of concernfully
            Being-out to get itself actualized
       780. 3. The significance of the possibility for
            the understanding of Being-towards-death
p.306 781. 4. Expecting as problem of Dasein's comport-
            ment towards something possible in its
            possibility
       782. 5. Being-towards death as anticipation of a
            possibility and as the possibility of
            any existence at all
p.307 783. Death as ownmost and uttermost possibility
       of authentic existence and the anticipation
       of death:
       784. 1. Death as Dasein's ownmost possibility
p.308 785. 2. The non-relational character of death as
            Dasein's ownmost possibility

S.264 786. 3. Die Unüberholbarkeit des Todes als eigenste, unbezügliche Möglichkeit des Daseins
787. 4. Die Gewissheit des Todes als eigenste,
unbezügliche und unüberholbare Möglichkeit des Daseins:
a) Gewissheit des Todes und Gewissheit
als Evidenz über Vorhandenes
S.265 788. b) Das Wesen der Gewissheit des Todes
789. 5. Die unbestimmte Gewissheit des Todes als
eigenste, unbezügliche, unüberholbare
und gewisse Möglichkeit des Daseins
S.266 790. Zusammenfassung über die Charakteristik des
existenzial entworfenen eigentlichen Seins
zum Tode
791. Das Vorlaufen in den Tod als ontologische
Möglichkeit und das Problem eines existenziellen eigentlichen Seins zum Tode
S.267 792 Methodische Erwägungen:
1. Bezüglich des vom Dasein aus dem Grunde
seines Seins geforderten und durch das
Vorlaufen bestimmten eigentlichen Seinkönnens
793. 2. Bezüglich der phänomenalen Grundlage für
die Frage nach dem eigentlichen Ganzsein
des Daseins und dessen existenzialer Verfassung

Kapitel 2

DIE DASEINSMÄSSIGE BEZEUGUNG EINES
EIGENTLICHEN SEINKÖNNENS UND DIE
ENTSCHLOSSENHEIT (S.267-301)

54. Das Problem der Bezeugung einer
eigentlichen existenziellen Möglichkeit
(S.267-270)

S.267 794. Methodische Erwägungen:
1. Zum Problem der Bezeugung einer eigentlichen existenziellen Möglichkeit des
Daseins
795. 2. Über eigentliches Selbstseinkönnen

p.308 786. 3. The character of death which is "not to
be outstripped" as Dasein's ownmost,
non-relational possibility
p.309 787. 4. Certainty of death as Dasein's ownmost,
non-relational character, which is not
to be outstripped:
a) Certainty of death and certainty as
evidence about the present-at-hand
788. b) The nature of the certainty of death
p.310 789. 5. The indefinite certainty of death as
Dasein's ownmost, non-relational, and
certain possibility, which is not to be
outstripped
p.311 790. Summary of the characterization of authentic Being-towards-death as it has been pro-
jected existentially
791. Anticipation of death as ontological possibility and as problem of an existentiell
Being-towards-death which is authentic
792. Methodical considerations:
1. About Dasein's demand, even by reason
of its ownmost Being, of an authentic
potentiality-for-Being determined by
anticipation
793. 2. About the consequences for the question
of Dasein's authentic Being-whole and
its existential constitution

Chapter II

DASEIN'S ATTESTATION OF AN AUTHENTIC
POTENTIALITY-FOR-BEING, AND RESOLUTENESS
(pp.312-348)

54. The Problem of How an Authentic
Existentiell Possibility is Attested
(pp.312-315)

p.312 794. Methodical considerations:
1. About the problem of an authentic
potentiality-for-Being of Dasein which
will be attested in its existential
possibility by Dasein itself
795. 2. About the authentic potentiality-for-
Being-one's-self

S.268 796. Sichentscheiden als Seinkönnen aus dem eigenen Selbst und als Sichzurückholen aus der
existenziellen Modifikation des Man-selbst
797. Das Dasein und sein Bedürfnis der Bezeugung
eines Selbstseinkönnens
798. Methodische Erwägungen zum Phänomen des Gewissens:
1. Die Stimme des Gewissens
799. 2. Abgrenzung der ontologischen Analyse des
Gewissens
S.269 800. 3. Die Tatsächlichkeit des Gewissens
801. 4. Gewissen und Erschlossenheit des Daseins
802. Methodische Erwägungen zur Anlage von Kapitel 2 und dessen thematischer Gliederung

55. Die existenzial-ontologischen
Fundamente des Gewissens   (S.270-272)

S.270 803. Das Gewissen und sein Zusammenhang mit den
das Sein des Da als Erschlossenheit konsti-
tuierenden existenzialen Phänomenen
804. Gewissen als Angerufenwerden des Daseins
und als Bruch des Daseins mit seinem Hinhö-
ren auf das Man
S.271 805. Das Rufen des Gewissens als Erschliessungs-
tendenz
806. Abgrenzung des Rufes des Gewissens und seines Ursprungs im Modus der Rede

56. Der Rufcharakter des Gewissens
(S.272-274)

S.272 807. Das Beredete als Bestandteil der Rede
808. Das Man-selbst als das im Ruf des Gewissens
Beredete und Angerufene
S.273 809. Das Angerufenwerden des Man-selbst als ein
Zu-ihm-selbst-bringen des Selbst
810. Der Anruf des Gewissens und das "Innenleben"
811. Der Anruf des Gewissens als Aufruf zum eigensten Seinkönnen des Selbst
812. Das im Modus des Schweigens sich vollziehen-
de Reden des Gewissens
S.274 813. Die Eindeutigkeit des Rufes des Gewissens
und Gründe für das Verfehlen des Rufes
814. Zusammenfassung über den Ruf des Gewissens

p.312 796. Deciding as making this decision from one's own Self for a potentiality-for-Being and as bringing oneself back from an existentiell manner in which the "they" is modified

p.313 797. Dasein and its need for having a potentiality-for-Being-its-Self

798. Methodical Considerations about the phenomenon of the conscience:
     1. The voice of conscience

799. 2. Demarcation of the ontological analysis of the conscience

800. 3. The factuality of the conscience

p.314 801. 4. Conscience and disclosedness of Dasein

802. Methodical considerations about the arrangement of the main themes in chapter 2

     55. The Existential-ontological
         Foundations of Conscience
             (pp.315-317)

p.315 803. Conscience and its interconnection with the existential phenomena which constitute the Being of the "there" as disclosedness

804. Conscience as Dasein's "being appealed to" and as Dasein's breaking off its listening away to the "they"

p.316 805. The calling of conscience as tendency to disclosure

806. Demarcation of the call of conscience and of its origin in the mode of discourse

     56. The Character of Conscience
         as a Call (pp.317-319)

p.317 807. That which is talked about as item of discourse

808. The they-self as that which in the call of conscience is talked about and to which is made an appeal

809. The appeal to the they-self as the bringing-to-its-Self of the Self

p.318 810. The call of the conscience and "inner life"

811. The appeal of the conscience as summons to the ownmost potentiality-for-Being-its-Self

812. The discoursing of the conscience in the mode of keeping silent

813. The unequivocalness of the call of the conscience and reasons for missing this call

p.319 814. Summary of the call of the conscience

S.274 815. Methodische Erwägungen über eine ontologisch zureichende Interpretation des Gewissens

57. Das Gewissen als Ruf der Sorge
(S.274-280)

S.274 816. Zusammenfassung über die Unbestimmtheit und
Unbestimmbarkeit des Rufers im Gewissen
S.275 817. Methodische Erwägungen über den Weg zur Erfassung des Rufers im Gewissen:
818. 1. Ursprung und Ziel des Rufers
819. 2. Methodische Voreiligkeit über den Rufer
im Gewissen bei biologischer und theolo-
gischer Erklärung
820. 3. Das Phänomen des Rufers des Gewissens
und seine Vorzeichnung im Dasein
S.276 821. 4. Die Faktizität des Daseins als durch ein
in die Existenz-Geworfensein bestimmtes
Seiendes
822. 5. Unheimlichkeit, Angst und elementarste
Erschlossenheit des Daseins
823. Das im Grunde seiner Unheimlichkeit sich be-
findende Dasein als der Rufer des Gewissens-
rufes
824. Der Rufer als das in der Unheimlichkeit auf
sich vereinzelte und in das Nichts geworfe-
ne Selbst
S.277 825. Die schlechthinnige Unverwechselbarkeit des
in seiner Unheimlichkeit auf sich vereinzel-
ten Daseins als Ziel des Rufers
826. Die Unheimlichkeit als Grundart des In-der-
Welt-seins und die durch diese bedrohte
selbstvergessene Verlorenheit des Daseins
827. Das Gewissen als Ruf der Sorge und die ge-
nauere Kennzeichnung dieses Phänomens
S.278 828. Der Grund für die "abwegigen" Erklärungen
des Gewissens als eine der nichtdaseinsmäs-
sigen Mächte
829. Das sogenannte "öffentliche Gewissen" als
Flucht vor dem Gewissen und als Stimme des
Man
830. Das "Weltgewissen" und die Jemeinigkeit des
Gewissens

p.319 815. Methodical considerations about an ontologically adequate interpretation of the
conscience

57. Conscience as the Call of
   Care (pp.319-325)

p.319 816. Summary of the caller of the conscience in
relation to its indefiniteness and vague-
ness
p.320 817. Methodical considerations about the way to
be followed for conceiving the caller of
the conscience:
     818. 1. Origin and goal of the caller
     819. 2. Biological and theological explanations
        about the caller of the conscience and
        their methodical precipitation
     820. 3. The phenomenon of the caller of the con-
        science and its ontological delineation
        in Dasein
     821. 4. Dasein's facticity as an entity deter-
        mined by Being-thrown-into-existence
p.321 822. 5. Uncanniness, anxiety, and Dasein's most
        elemental disclosedness
     823. Dasein as the caller of the call of con-
        science finding itself in the very depth of
        its uncanniness
     824. The caller as the Self which has been indi-
        vidualized down to itself in uncanniness and
        been thrown into the nothing
p.322 825. Dasein individualized down to itself in un-
        canniness as characterization of the goal
        of the caller is for itself something that
        cannot be mistaken for anything else
     826. Uncanniness -- the threat to the lostness
        in which Dasein has forgotten itself
     827. Conscience as the call of conscience and a
        more explicite characterization of this
        phenomenon
p.323 828. The conscience seen as one of the powers
        with a character other than that of Dasein
        and reasons why these explanations have
        gone off the track
     829. The so-called public conscience as escape
        from the conscience and as voice of the
        "they"
     830. World-conscience and the mineness of the
        conscience

103

S.278 831. Die Bedeutsamkeit der Interpretation des
Gewissens als des Rufers

S.279 832. Methodische Erwägungen:
1. Bezüglich der Bedenken über die bisherige Interpretation des Gewissens und der
damit verbundenen Probleme

833. 2. Über die Vorläufigkeit der bisherigen
Analyse des Gewissens als Vorbereitung
der Aufgabe der genauen Kennzeichnung
des Gewissens

834. 3. Bezüglich des Problems des richtigen Zu-
gangs zu dem von dem Gewissen Bezeugten

835. 4. Über die Notwendigkeit der Analyse des
Anrufverstehens zum Verstehen des im Ruf
Enthaltenen

58. Anrufverstehen und Schuld
(S.280-289)

S.280 836. Methodische Erwägungen:
1. Über das Anrufen des Man-selbst als Aufruf und den methodischen Ansatz für die
existenziale Interpretation dessen, wozu
der Ruf aufruft

837. 2. Über das Problem der Eigentlichkeit bezüglich des existenziell-hörenden Verstehens des Rufes

838. 3. Über das wesenhaft in der Eigentlichkeit
des Anrufverstehens Gegebene

839. 4. Über Schuldigsein als Gegebenes

S.281 840. 5. Bezüglich des methodischen Ansatzes zur
Gewinnung eines existenzialen Begriffes
des Schuldigseins

841. Die alltägliche Verständigkeit des Schuldigseins:
1. Als schulden

S.282 842. 2. Als schuld sein

843. 3. Als schuldig machen

844. Methodische Erwägungen:
1. Über das Schuldigsein als Seinsart des
Daseins und seine ontologische Abgrenzung vom Begriff der sittlichen Schuld

S.283 845. 2. Bezüglich der Klärung des Schuldphäno-
mens

846. 3. Über die Formalisierung der Idee des
Schuldigseins und ihre Ablösung vom Bezug auf ein Sollen oder ein Gesetz

p.323 831. The significance of the interpretation of
the conscience as caller
832. Methodical considerations:
1. About doubts concerning the preceding
interpretation of the conscience and
the problems related to it
p.324 833. 2. About the provisionalness of the preceding analysis of the conscience as prepa-
ration for the task of an explicite
characterization of the conscience
834. 3. About the problem of the right access to
that which conscience attests to
835. 4. About the necessity of an analysis of the
understanding of the appeal as understanding the content of the call

58. Understanding the Appeal,
and Guilt (pp.325-335)

p.325 836. Methodical considerations:
1. About the appeal to the they-self as
summons and the methodical point of departure of the existential interpretation
of that towards which the call summons
us
837. 2. About the problem of authenticity with
regard to understanding the call with an
existentiell kind of hearing
838. 3. About that which is essentially given
when the call is understood authentically
p.326 839. 4. About Being-guilty as something given
840. 5. About the methodical basis for establish-
ing an existential conception of Being-
guilty
p.327 841. Everyday common sense and its understanding
of Being-guilty:
1. As having debts
842. 2. As being responsible for
843. 3. As making oneself responsible
p.328 844. Methodical considerations:
1. About Being-guilty as a kind of Being of
Dasein and its ontological distinction
from the concept of moral guilt
845. 2. About clarifying the phenomenon of guilt
846. 3. About the formalizing of the idea of
Being-guilty and its being detached
from a relationship to any law or "ought"

105

S.283 847. 4. Über das Schuldigsein als ein ursprüng-
lich mit der Existenz gegebenes Grund-
sein einer Nichtigkeit
S.284 848. Dasein als Sorge und das Wesen der damit
verbundenen Geworfenheit
849. Das Dasein als geworfener Grund
850. Das Grundsein des Daseins:
1. Das Nie-mächtig-sein des Daseins als
sein eigenstes Sein von Grund auf
S.285 851. 2. Die wesenhafte Nichtigkeit des Entwurfs
als existenziales Konstitutivum der
Seinsstruktur des Entwerfens
852. Die Sorge als geworfener Entwurf und dessen
Bedeutung als Nichtigkeit und Schuldigsein
853. Das Kennzeichnende der existenzialen Nichtigkeit
854. Das Problem des ontologischen Wesens des
Nicht überhaupt und seine bisherige Vernachlässigung in der Philosophie
S.286 855. Die Unzulänglichkeit der Begriffe "Privation" und "Mangel" für die ontologische Interpretation des Nicht und des Schuldphäno-
mens
856. Wesenhaftes Schuldigsein als gleichursprüng-
liche existenziale Bedingung der Möglichkeit für Moralität überhaupt
857. Der Vorrang des Schuldigseins vor dem Wis-
sen um das Schuldigsein
858. Das Schuldigsein als das Konstitutivum der
Sorge
S.287 859. Mögliches Missverstehen des Schuldigseins
des Daseins
860. Der Sinn von "Aufrufen zum Schuldigsein":
861. 1. Die Übernahme des Schuldigseins als
eigentliches Sein des Daseins
862. 2. Die Öffnung des Daseins zu seiner eigensten Existenzmöglichkeit
S.288 863. Anrufverstehen als Gewissen-haben-wollen:
864. 1. Abgrenzung des Gewissen-haben-wollens gegenüber dem vulgären Verständnis von
Schuld
865. 2. Gewissen-haben-wollen und faktisches
Schuldigwerden
866. Methodische Erwägungen:
1. Über das Gewissen als ein zum Sein des
Daseins gehörende Bezeugung

p.329 847. 4. About Being-guilty as primordial Being-
the-bias of the nullity which is given
with existence
848. Dasein as care and the nature of thrownness
which is connected with care
p.330 849. Dasein as its own basis
850. Dasein's Being-a-basis:
1. Dasein's Being as "never to have power
over" its ownmost Being from the ground
up
p.331 851. 2. The essential nullity of the projection
as that which is existentially constitutive for the structure of the Being of
projection
852. Care as thrown projection and the meaning
of projection as nullity and Being-guilty
853. The characteristics of existential nullity
854. The problem of the ontological nature of
the "not" in general and its customary
neglect in philosophical studies
p.332 855. The insufficiency of the concepts of "privation" and "lack" for an ontological interpretation of the "not" and the phenomenon
of guilt
856. Essentially Being-guilty as equiprimordially
existential condition for the possibility
of morality in general
857. The priority of Being-guilty over knowing
about Being-guilty
858. Being-guilty as constituting care
p.333 859. The problem of a possible misunderstanding
of Dasein's Being-guilty
860. The meaning of the summons to Being-guilty:
861. 1. The acceptance of Being-guilty as
authentic Being
862. 2. Dasein's opening to its ownmost possibility of existence
p.334 863. Understanding the appeal as wanting to have
a conscience:
864. 1. "Wanting to have a conscience" and its
distinction from the ordinary understanding of guilt
865. 2. "Wanting to have a conscience" and
factically coming to owe something
866. Methodical considerations:
1. About the conscience as an attestation
which belongs to Dasein's Being

S.288 867. 2. Über den Zusammenhang von Ergebnissen
der ontologischen Analyse mit den alltäglichen Gewissenserfahrungen

59. Die existenziale Interpretation
des Gewissens und die vulgäre
Gewissensauslegung (S.289-295)

S.289 868. Existenziale und vulgäre Auslegung des Gewissens
869. Methodische Erwägungen:
1. Über das Problem einer notwendigen Übereinstimmung beider Auslegungen des Gewissens
870. 2. Über die notwendige Übereinstimmung von
existenzialem und vulgärem Verständnis
des Gewissens
S.290 871. Die vier grundsätzlichen Einwände der vulgären Gewissensauslegung gegen die existenziale Gewissensauslegung:
872. 1. Vernachlässigung der Grundformen des Gewissens:
a) Böses Gewissen:
1) Das Erlebnis des bösen Gewissens
873. 2) Das Problematische der Auslegung
des bösen Gewissens als Schuldigsein
S.291 874. b) Gutes Gewissen:
1) Das Erlebnis des guten Gewissens
875. 2) Die Fragwürdigkeit von Max Schelers Interpretation des guten Gewissens als Privation des bösen
Gewissens
S.292 876. 3) Der nichtexistenziale Charakter
des guten Gewissens
877. c) Das Erlebnis des vorweisend-warnenden
und des rückweisend-rügenden Gewissens
878. 2. Das Problem der wurzelhaften Bezogenheit
der Stimme des Gewissens:
a) Das Nichtkennen eines Aufgerufenwer-
dens zum Schuldigsein seitens der
alltäglichen Gewissenserfahrung

p.335 867. 2. About the connection between the results
of the ontological analysis and the
everyday ways in which the conscience
is experienced

59. The Existential Interpretation
of the Conscience, and the Way
Conscience is Ordinarily Inter-
preted (pp.335-341)

p.335 868. Existential and ordinary interpretation
of the conscience
869. Methodical considerations:
1. About the problem of a necessary agreement of these two interpretations of the
conscience
p.336 870. 2. About the necessary agreement between
existential and ordinary understanding
of the conscience
871. The four principal objections of the ordinary interpretation of the conscience to
the existential interpretation:
872. 1. Neglect of the basic forms of the
conscience:
a) The evil conscience:
(1) The experience of the evil
conscience
p.337 873. (2) The problematics of the interpretation of the evil conscience as
Being-guilty
874. b) The good conscience:
(1) The experience of the good conscience
p.338 875. (2) The dubiousness of Max Scheler's
interpretation of the good con-
science as a privation of the
evil conscience
876. (3) The non-existential character of
the good conscience
877. c) The experience of a conscience which
points forward and warns, and one
which points back and reproves
p.339 878. 2. The voice of the conscience and the
problem of its radical relation to
Dasein's Being:
a) The lack of acquaintance with anything like getting summoned to Being-
guilty as far as everyday experiences
of the conscience is concerned

109

S.293 879. 2. b) Die Gewissensinterpretation bei Kant
und in der Werttheorie
880.   c) Erwägungen über die alltägliche Gewissenserfahrung
881 3. Das Gewissen als Sprecher auf eine bestimmte vollzogene oder gewollte Tat
882. 4. Das Gewissen als kritische Funktion:
a) Das Erlebnis der kritischen Funktion
des Gewissens
S.294 883.   b) Das Problem des Wesens des positiven
Gehaltes des im Gewissen Gerufenen
884. Ergebnis der Untersuchung über die vulgäre
Gewissensauslegung
S.295 885. Ursprüngliches existenziales Gewissensver-
ständnis und existenzielle Gewissenserfahrung

60. Die existenziale Struktur des
im Gewissen bezeugten eigentlichen
Seinkönnens (S.295-301)

S.295 886. Eigentliches Rufverstehen des Gewissens als
eine Weise der Erschlossenheit des Daseins
887. Die Wesensmomente der Erschlossenheit des
Daseins:
1. Existenzielles Verstehen als ein Entwerfen auf das eigentliche Seinkönnen
888. 2. Die Befindlichkeit der Angst
S.296 889. 3. Die Rede als Verschwiegenheit
890. Die Verdeckung der schweigenden Rede des
Gewissens durch das Man
891. Entschlossenheit als ausgezeichneter Modus
der Erschlossenheit des Daseins
S.297 892. Existenziale Interpretation der Erschlossenheit als ursprüngliche Wahrheit
893. Die Kennzeichnung der Entschlossenheit als
der eigentlichen Wahrheit des Daseins
S.298 894. Entschlossenheit als eigentliches In-der-
Welt-sein und als eigentliches Selbstsein
895. Das eigentliche Selbstsein der Erschlossenheit als Möglichkeit für die Gewährung des
eigentlichen Selbstseins des Anderen

p.339 879.   b) The interpretation of the conscience as presented by Kant and by the theory of value

880.   c) Considerations about the everyday experience of conscience

881. 3. The conscience as speaking in a way that is relative to some definite deed which has been performed or willed

p.340 882. 4. The assumption that the function of the conscience be essentially critical:
    a) The experience of the critical function of the conscience

883.   b) The problem of the nature of the positive content in that which is called in the conscience

p.341 884. Results of the investigation about the ordinary interpretation of the conscience

885. Primordial existential understanding of the conscience and existentiell experience of the conscience

60. The Existential Structure of the Authentic Potentiality-for-Being which is Attested in the Conscience (pp.341-348)

p.341 886. The authentic understanding of the call of the conscience as a way in which Dasein has been disclosed

p.342 887. The essential items of Dasein's disclosedness:
    1. Understanding in an existentiell manner as projecting oneself upon one's ownmost potentiality-for-Being

888. 2. The state-of-mind of anxiety

889. 3. Discourse as reticence

p.343 890 The silent discourse of the conscience and its being covered up by the "they"

891. Resoluteness as a distinctive mode of Dasein's disclosedness

892. Disclosedness and its existential interpretation as being the primordial truth

893. The characteristic of resoluteness as Dasein's authentic truth

p.344 894. Resoluteness as authentically Being-in-the-world and as authentically Being-one's-Self

895. Authentic Being-one's-Self in resoluteness as possibility for granting Others their authentic Being-one's-Self

S.298 896. Der Entschluss als erschliessendes Entwer-
          fen und Bestimmen der jeweiligen fakti-
          schen Möglichkeit des Daseins
      897. Entschlossenheit als Sich-aufrufen-lassen
          aus der Verlorenheit in das Man und das
          existenziale Phänomen der Situation
S.299 898. Die Charakterisierung der Situation
S.300 899. Das Man und die Situation
      900. Der Gewissensruf als Aufruf zum Seinkönnen
          und als Vorruf in die Situation
      901. Charakterisierung der Entschlossenheit als
          mögliche Eigentlichkeit der Sorge und ihre
          Abgrenzung zum Handeln
S.301 902. Methodische Erwägungen:
          1. Bezüglich der Interpretation der existen-
             zialen Strukturen faktischer existen-
             zieller Möglichkeiten
      903. 2. Über die weitere Untersuchung des eigent-
             lichen Ganzseinkönnens des Daseins

Kapitel 3

DAS EIGENTLICHE GANZSEINKÖNNEN DES
DASEINS UND DIE ZEITLICHKEIT ALS DER
ONTOLOGISCHE SINN DER SORGE   (S.301-333)

61. Vorzeichnung des methodischen
Schrittes von der Umgrenzung des
eigentlichen daseinsmässigen Ganzseins
zur phänomenalen Freilegung der
Zeitlichkeit (S.301-305)

S.301 904. Das Problem der Untersuchung des Ganzseins
          des Daseins
S.302 905. Aufweis eines möglichen Zusammenhanes von
          Vorlaufen zum Tode und Entschlossenheit
      906. Methodische Erwägungen:
          1. Über existenziale Interpretation und die
             Idee der Existenz
S.303 907. 2. Über den Gang der gesamten Untersuchung
      908. Das Kennzeichen echter methodischer Besin-
          nung und die existenziale Analytik
      909. Dasein, Sorge und das Phänomen des Selbst

p.345 896. Resoluteness as disclosive projection and determination of what for Dasein is possible at the time

897. Resoluteness as letting oneself be summoned out of one's lostness in the "they" and the existential phenomenon of the Situation

p.346 898. Characterization of the Situation

899. The "they" and the Situation

p.347 900. The call of conscience as summons to our potentiality-for-Being and as calling us forth into the Situation

901. The characterizing of resoluteness as possible authenticity of care itself and the distinction between care and taking action

p.348 902. Methodical considerations:
1. Concerning the interpretation of existential structures of factical existentiell possibilities

903. 2. About the following continuing investigation into Dasein's authentic potentiality-for Being-a-whole

Chapter III

DASEIN'S AUTHENTIC POTENTIALITY-FOR-
BEING-A-WHOLE, AND TEMPORALITY AS
THE ONTOLOGICAL MEANING OF CARE
(pp.349-382)

60. A Preliminare Sketch of the
Methodological Step from the Definition
of Dasein's Authentic Being-a-whole to
the Laying-bare of Temporality as
a Phenomenon (pp.349-352)

p.349 904. The problem of the investigation of Dasein's Being-a-whole

905. Exhibition of a possible connection between anticipation of death and resoluteness

p.350 906. Methodical considerations:
1. About existential interpretation and the idea of existence

907. 2. About the course of the total investigation in Martin Heidegger's treatise

908. The characteristics of a genuine methodical consideration and the existential analytic

p.351 909. Dasein, care, and the phenomenon of the Self

S.303   910. Vorausgreifende Zusammenfassung über den
             ontologischen Sinn der Sorge und die
             Freilegung der Zeitlichkeit
S.304   911. Methodische Erwägungen:
             1. Über die Zeitlichkeit und den vulgären
             Zeitbegriff
        912. 2. Bezüglich der thematischen Entfaltung
             der zu behandelnden Themen über das
             ursprüngliche Phänomen der Zeitlich-
             keit

        62. Das existenziell eigentliche
        Ganzseinkönnen des Daseins als
   vorlaufende Entschlossenheit   (S.305-310)

S.305   913. Die eigenste Seinstendenz der Entschlos-
             senheit als auf das eigentliche Sein-zum-
             Tode führend und die damit verbundenen
             Probleme
        914. Entschlossenheit und das in ihr sich ber-
             gende eigentliche Sein-zum-Tode als die
             mögliche existenzielle Modalität der der
             Entschlossenheit eigenen Eigentlichkeit
        915. Entschlossenheit als das Sichvorrufenlas-
             sen auf das eigenste Schuldigsein
S.306   916. Vorläufige Entschlossenheit als eigentli-
             ches Seinkönnen der Sorge und zwar als
             Gleichursprünglichkeit der Bergung von
             Tod und Schuld in der Sorge
S.307   917. Das Verstehen des Seins-zum-Tode als ei-
             genste Möglichkeit des eigenen Seinkönnens
        918. Der Ruf des Gewissens und die vorlaufende
             Entschlossenheit
        919. Kennzeichnung der Unverdecktheit des vor-
             läufigen und ständigen Schuldigseins
        920. Die Gewissheit der Entschlossenheit als
             Offenheit und als ursprüngliche Wahrheit
             der Existenz
S.308   921. Das Geworfensein in die Grenzsituation
             als das Offensein des Daseins für seine
             ständige mögliche Verlorenheit in die Un-
             entschlossenheit des Man, die eine Verlo-
             renheit in die Unwahrheit ist
S.309   922. Ergebnis der Analyse des Zusammenhanges
             von "Sein-zum-Tode" und "Entschlossen-
             heit":
        923. 1. Existenziales Verständnis des Vorlau-
             fens

114

p.351   910. Forestalling summary about the ontological meaning of care and the laying-bare
of temporality

p.352   911. Methodical considerations:
      1. About temporality and the ordinary
concept of time
912. 2. About the arrangement of the main
themes of chapter 3 concerning the
primordial phenomenon of temporality

62. Anticipatory Resoluteness as the
Way in which Dasein's Potentiality-for-
Being-a-whole has Existentiell
Authenticity (pp.352-358)

p.352   913. The problems which are related to the
ownmost tendency of the Being of resoluteness and its leading to authentic
Being-towards-death

p.353   914. The authentic Being-towards-death which
resoluteness harbours in itself as the
possible existentiell modality of its
own authenticity

915. Resoluteness as letting oneself be called
forth to one's ownmost Being-guilty

p.354   916. Anticipatory resoluteness as the ownmost
potentiality-for-Being of care, namely
as harbouring in itself both death and
guilt equiprimordially

917. The understanding of Being-towards-death
as one's ownmost possibility of one's
potentiality-for-Being

918. The call of conscience and anticipatory
resoluteness

919. Characterization of that which is uncon-
cealed of the prior and constant Being-
guilty

p.355   920. The certainty of resoluteness as openness
and as primordial truth of existence

p.356   921. Being-thrown into the limit-Situation as
Dasein's openness for its constant possible lostness in the irresoluteness of
the "they", which is a Being-lost in the
untruth

922. Results of the analysis of the connection
between Being-towards-death and resoluteness:

923a/b [923b on p.357] 1. The existential understanding of anticipation

S.309   (924.) 2. Existenziales und existenzielles
                eigentliches Ganzseinkönnen des Daseins
        925. 3. Die Aufweisung eines eigentlichen Ganz-
                seinkönnens des Daseins
S.310   926. 4. Die Grundstimmungen der vorlaufenden
                Entschlossenheit des Daseins
        927. Methodische Erwägungen über die in Ab-
                schnitt 62 durchgeführte ontologische In-
                terpretation der Existenz des Daseins

        63. Die für eine Interpretation des
            Seinssinnes der Sorge gewonnene
            hermeneutische Situation und der
    methodische Charakter der existenzialen
            Analytik überhaupt (S.310-316)

S.310   928. Zusammenfassung über das phänomenale
             Sichtbarmachen des Daseins hinsichtlich
             seiner möglichen Eigentlichkeit und Ganz-
             heit:
             1. Allgemeines Ergebnis
S.311   929. 2. "Das Seiende, das wir selbst sind, ist
                das ontologisch Fernste" als die Grund-
                these der existenzialen Analytik
        930. 3. Die existenziale Analyse und das durch
                besorgende Verständigkeit des Seinkön-
                nens Verschliessen des Daseins
        931. Die eigene Verdeckungstendenz des Seins
                des Daseins und die gegen diese als Er-
                oberung durchzuführende ontologische In-
                terpretation
S.312   932. Existenziale Analytik und Selbstauslegung
                als Wesensmoment des Seins des Daseins
        933. Das Problem der in der existenzialen Ana-
                lytik angesetzten Idee der Existenz:
                1. Das Problem des Kriteriums für die
                eigentliche Existenz des Daseins
S.313   934. 2. Das Problem der methodischen Vorgabe
                von Möglichkeiten der Existenz
        935. 3. Das Problem der vorgesetzten Existenz-
                idee

116

p.357   (924) 2. Existentially and existentielly authen-
                tic potentiality-for-Being-a-whole
         925. 3. The exhibiting of an authentic poten-
                tiality-for-Being-a-whole which belongs
                to Dasein
         926. 4. The basic moods of the anticipatory
                resoluteness of Dasein
p.358   927. Methodical considerations about that in-
                terpretation of Dasein's existence which
                has been carried out in section 62

            63. The Hermeneutical Situation at
       which we have Arrived for Interpreting
        the Meaning of the Being of Care; and
         the Methodological Character of the
           Existential Analytic in General
                   (pp.358-364)

p.358   928. Summary about Dasein's having phenomenal-
                ly made visible with regard to its pos-
                sible authenticity and totality:
                1. General results
P.359   929. 2. The proposition "The entity which in
                every case we ourselves are, is onto-
                logically that which is farthest" as
                the basic thesis of the existential
                analytic
         930. 3. Existential analytic and the closing
                off of Dasein by means of concernful
                common sense
         931. Dasein's own tendency to cover things up
                and the ontological interpretation as
                capture which has to be carried out
                against this tendency
p.360   932. Existential analytic and the interpreta-
                tion of the Self as essential item of
                Dasein's Being
         933. The problem of the idea of existence
                which has been postulated in existential
                analytic:
                1. The problem of the criterion for Da-
                sein's authentic existence
         934. 2. The problem of the method and the
                presentation of possibilities of
                existence
p.361   935. 3. The problem of the presupposed idea
                of existence

S.313   936. Die angesetzte Existenzidee als existen-
ziell unverbindliche Vorzeichnung der formalen Struktur des Daseinsverständnisses
überhaupt

S.314   937. Die angesetzte Existenzidee als das die
existenziale Analytik leitende Kriterium

938. Existenzidee, Existenz und Realität

939. Existenziale Analytik und das Problem des
Zirkels

940. Das Problem des Zirkels als das Problem
der Notwendigkeit von Voraussetzungen

S.315   941. Verständigkeit als Grundlage des Zirkel-
einwandes und als besorgendes Aufgehen im
Man

942. Die Klärung des existenzialen Sinnes der
hermeneutischen Situation einer ursprünglichen Analytik des Daseins

S.316   943. Methodische Erwägungen über existenziale
Analyse

944. Die Erschlossenheit des Seinssinnes der
Sorge als die ursprünglichste, grundlegen-
de existenziale Wahrheit

64. Sorge und Selbstheit (S.316-323)

S.316   945. Zusammenfassung:
1. Über die Sorgestruktur und die Einheit
ihrer konstitutiven Momente als Bedingung der Möglichkeit eines eigentlichen
Ganzseinkönnens des Daseins

S.317   946. 2. Über die Einheit des Strukturganzen
der Sorge und das Problem des Ich als
eigentlichem Selbst

S.318   947. Die ontische Erfahrung des Ich bei Kant

948. Die ontologische Basis der Kantischen Analyse des Ich-sagens

S.319   949. Kants Analyse der transzendentalen Apper-
zeption

950. Der phänomenale Gehalt des Ich bei Kant

951. Kritik an Kants Ansatz des Ich

S.320   952. Gründe für Kants Rückfall zum Ich als
Substanziale:
1. Allgemeine Erwägungen

p.361   936. The idea of existence which has been posited as an existentielly nonbinding sketch of the formal structure of Dasein's understanding in general

937. The idea of existence which has been posited as the guiding criterion for the existential analytic

p.362   938. Existence, reality, and the idea of existence

939. The existential analytic and the problem of the circle

940. The problem of circularity as that of the necessity of presuppositions

p.363   941. Common sense as the foundation for the charge of circularity and as concernful absorption in the "they"

942. The clarifying of the existential meaning of the hermeneutical Situation of a primordial analytic of Dasein

p.364   943. Methodical considerations about the existential analytic

944. The disclosedness of the meaning of the Being of care as the most primordial and basic existential truth

64. Care and Selfhood (pp.364-370)

p.364   945. Summary:
1. About the care-structure and the unity of its constitutive items as the condition for Dasein's authentic potentiality-for-Being-a-whole

p.365   946. 2. About the unity of care as a structural whole and about the problem of the "I" as authentic Self

p.366   947. The way in which Kant understands the ontical experience of the "I"

948. The ontological foundation for saying "I" in Kant's analysis

949. Kant's analysis of transcendental apperception

p.367   950. The phenomenal content of the "I" in Kant's manner of thinking

951. Criticism of the foundation of Kant's postulation of the "I"

952. Reasons for Kant to fall back on seeing the "I" as a substance:
1. General considerations

S.321   953. Kants Nichtbeachtung des In-der-Welt-
seins des Daseins

954. Das Ich-sagen und die alltägliche Selbstauslegung des Ich

S.322   955. Die Motivierung des "flüchtigen" Ich-sagens in der Ich-Rede des Besorgens

956. Zusammenfassung über die ontologische Interpretation des Ich

957. Das eigentliche Selbst des Daseins

S.323   958. Die die Sorge konstituierende Existenzialität als Grundlage für die Verfassung
der Selbst-ständigkeit des Daseins

65. Die Zeitlichkeit als der ontologische Sinn der Sorge (S.323-331)

S.323   959. Methodische Erwägungen über das Wesentli-
che des Daseins

960. Das Kennzeichen des Sinnes

S.324   961. Methodische Erwägungen über das Freilegen
des Sinnes

962. Sinn als das Woraufhin des primären Entwurfs des Verstehens von Sein

963. Sinn als das in seinem Sein zugänglich
gewordene Seiende

S.325   964. Der Seinssinn des Daseins als das sich
verstehende Dasein selbst

965. Die Zukunft als Ermöglichung des eigentlichen Ganzseins des Daseins hinsichtlich
der Einheit seines gegliederten Strukturganzen

966. Das Dasein und sein Zusammenhang mit seiner Gewesenheit

S.326   967. Die Gegenwart als Gegenwärtigen und das
Wesen der Entschlossenheit

968. Das Dasein als Zeitlichkeit

969. Abgrenzung der Zeitlichkeit von dem vulgären Zeitbegriff

S.327   970. Die Zeitlichkeit und die ursprüngliche
Einheit der Sorgestruktur

971. Die konstitutiven Momente der Sorge:
1. Die Zukunft als primärer Sinn der Existenzialität

S.328   972. 2. Gewesenheit als primär existenzialer
Sinn der Faktizität

p.367   953. 2. Kant's disregarding of Dasein's Being-
              in-the-world
p.368   954. Saying "I" and the everyday interpreta-
              tion with regard to the "I"
        955. The motivation of the "fugitive" way of
              saying "I" which is expressed in the
              talking of the "I" when it concerns it-
              self with something
        956a/b [956b on p.369]   Summary about the on-
              tological interpretation of the "I"
p.369   957. The authentic Self of Dasein
p.370   958. The existentiality which constitutes care
              as basis for the constitution of Dasein's
              Self-constancy

        65. Temporality as the Ontological
            Meaning of Care (pp.370-380)

p.370   959. Methodical considerations about that
              which is essential for Dasein
        960. Characterization of meaning
p.371   961. Methodical considerations about the
              laying-bare of meaning
        962. Meaning as the upon-which of the primary
              projection of the understanding of Being
        963. Meaning as entities which have become
              accessible in their Being
p.372   964. The meaning of Dasein as Dasein's self-
              understanding of itself
        965. The future as making possible the authen-
              tic Being-a-whole of Dasein with regard
              to its articulated structural whole
p.373   966. Dasein and its connection with the char-
              acter of having been [beenhood]
        967. The Present as making present the nature
              of resoluteness
p.374   968. Dasein as temporality
        969. Temporality as distinct from the ordinary
              concept of time
p.375   970. Temporality and the primordial structure
              of care
        971. The constitutive items of care:
              1. The future as the primary meaning of
              existentiality
p.376   972. 2. The character of having been as the
              primary existential meaning of facti-
              city

121

S.328   973. 3. Das Gegenwärtigen als primärer Grund
des Verfallens an das besorgte Zuhan-
dene und Vorhandene
974. Zeitlichkeit als Grundmöglichkeit der
eigentlichen und der uneigentlichen Existenz
975. Die Ekstasen der Zeitlichkeit und die ursprüngliche Zeit
S.329   976. Die Zukunft als das primäre Phänomen der
ursprünglichen und eigentlichen Zeitlichkeit
977. Die eigentliche primär die Zeitlichkeit
zeitigende Zukunft als endliche Zukunft
S.330   978. Die ursprüngliche Endlichkeit der Zeitlichkeit
979. Methodische Erwägungen über Endlichkeit
und Un-endlichkeit
S.331   980. Zusammenfassung über die Analyse der ursprünglichen Zeitlichkeit
981. Methodische Erwägungen bezüglich der weiteren Entfaltung der Untersuchung über
die Sorge als Zeitlichkeit

**66. Die Zeitlichkeit des Daseins und
die aus ihr entspringenden Aufgaben
einer ursprünglicheren Wiederholung
der existenzialen Analyse** (S.331-333)

S.331   982. Kennzeichnung der "zeitlichen" Interpretation
983. Methodische Erwägungen über die Analyse
der Uneigentlichkeit des Daseins in ihrer
spezifischen Zeitlichkeit
S.332   984. Die Zeitigungsstruktur der Zeitlichkeit
als die Geschichtlichkeit des Daseins
985. Innerzeitigkeit als Zeitbestimmtheit des
innerweltlichen Seienden
S.333   986. Methodische Erwägungen über die Ausarbeitung der Zeitlichkeit des Daseins als
Alltäglichkeit, Geschichtlichkeit und Innerzeitigkeit

p.376   973. 3. The making-present as the primary
               basis for falling into the ready-to-
               hand and the present-at-hand with which
               we concern ourselves
         974. Temporality as the basic possibility of
               authentic and inauthentic existence
p.377   975. The ecstases of temporality and primor-
               dial time
p.378   976. The future as the primary phenomenon of
               primordial and authentic temporality
         977. The authentic future which primarily
               temporalizes temporality as finite future
         978. The primordial finitude of temporality
p.379   979. Methodical considerations about finitude
               and in-finitude
p.380   980. Summary about the analysis of primordial
               temporality
         981. Methodical considerations about the ways
               of further investigating care as
               temporality

               66. Dasein's Temporality and the
               Tasks Arising Therefrom of Re-
               peating the Existential Anal-
               ysis in a more Primordial man-
               ner (pp.380-382)

p.380   982. Characterization of "the temporal inter-
               pretation"
         983. Methodical considerations about Dasein's
               inauthenticity and the own specific
               temporality of this inauthenticity
p.381   984. The temporalization-structure of tempo-
               rality as the historicality of Dasein
         985. Within-time-ness as the temporal attribute
               of entities within-the-world
p.382   986. Methodical considerations about working
               out the temporality of Dasein as every-
               dayness, historicality and within-time-
               ness

123

Kapitel 4

ZEITLICHKEIT UND ALLTÄGLICHKEIT
(S.334-372)

38. Der Grundbestand der existenzialen
Verfassung des Daseins und die
Vorzeichnung ihrer zeitlichen
Interpretation (S.334-335)

S.334   987. Die ursprüngliche Ganzheit der Daseins-
             verfassung als Mannigfaltigkeit
        988. Zusammenfassung über die aus der vorberei-
             tenden Analyse [S.41-230] gewonnenen Phä-
             nomene
        989. Vorzeichnung des weiteren Verlaufes der
             Ausarbeitung der zeitlichen Interpretation
             des alltäglichen Daseins
S.335   990. Gliederung von Kapitel 4

68. Die Zeitlichkeit der Erschlossenheit
überhaupt (S.335-350)

S.335   991. Methodische Erwägungen über die Ausarbei-
             tung des Aufweises der konkreten zeitli-
             chen Konstitution der Sorge

a) Die Zeitlichkeit des Verstehens
(S.336-339)

S.336   992. Verstehen und Erkennen
        993. Existenziales Fassen von Verstehen, Er-
             schlossenheit und Entschlossenheit
        994. Vorlaufen als terminologische Kennzeich-
             nung der eigentlichen Zukunft
S.337   995. Uneigentliches Verstehen und das Gewärti-
             gen als Kennzeichen der uneigentlichen
             Zukunft
        996. Der Augenblick als die in der Zeitlich-
             keit gehaltene eigentliche Gegenwart
S.338   997. Das Gegenwärtigen als uneigentliche Gegen-
             wart
        998. Wiederholung als eigentliche und Verges-
             senheit als uneigentliche Gewesenheit
S.339   999. Die Zusammenhänge von Erwartung und Gewär-
             tigen sowie von Erinnerung und Vergessen

Chapter IV

TEMPORALITY AND EVERYDAYNESS
(pp.383-423)

67. The Basic Content of Dasein's
Existential Constitution, and a
Preliminary Sketch of the Temporal
Interpretation of it (pp.383-384)

p.383   987. The primordial totality of Dasein's con-
              stitution as multiplicity of phenomena
         988. Summary of the phenomena which have been
              explored in the preparatory analysis
              [pp.65-273]
p.384   989. Sketch of the course which Martin Heideg-
              ger will take up for the working out of
              everyday Dasein's temporal interpretation
         990. Arrangement of the main themes of
              chapter 4

68. The Temporality of Disclosedness
in General (pp.384-401)

P.384   991. Methodical considerations about working
              out how to exhibit the concrete temporal
              constitution of care

(a) The Temporality of Understanding
(pp.385-389)

p.385   992. Understanding and Knowing
         993. The existential conceiving of understand-
              ing, disclosedness, and resoluteness
p.386   994. Anticipation as terminological designa-
              tion of the authentic future
         995. Inauthentic understanding and awaiting as
              characterization of inauthentic future
p.387   996. The "moment of vision" as that Present
              which is held in authentic temporality
p.388   997. Making present as inauthentic Present
         998. Repetition as the authentic way of "hav-
              ing been" [beenhood] and "having forgot-
              ten" as inauthentic way of "having been"
              [beenhood]
p.389   999. The Interconnectedness between expecting/
              awaiting and remembering/forgetting

b) Die Zeitlichkeit der Befindlichkeit

S.339   1000. Befindlichkeit und Geworfenheit
S.340   1001. Gewesenheit als die zeitliche Konstitu-
               tion der Gestimmtheit
        1002. Methodische Erwägungen über die existen-
               zial-zeitliche Konstitution der Gestimmt-
               heit
S.341   1003. Die Furcht als verwirrtes Gewärtigen und
               ihre Zeitigung aus dem Vergessen
S.342   1004. Die Zeitlichkeit der Furcht als gewärti-
               gend-gegenwärtigendes Vergessen
        1005. Die Angst als Ängsten vor dem Nichts der
               Welt
S.343   1006. Gewesenheit als die zeitliche Konstitu-
               tion der Angst und die in der Angst er-
               schlossene Unbedeutsamkeit der Welt
S.344   1007. Der Unterschied von Furcht und Angst
        1008. Die Möglichkeit der Angst und die Möglich-
               keit eines eigentlichen Seinkönnens des
               Daseins
        1009. Die sich aus je einem eigentümlichen Ver-
               stehen bestimmenden Stimmungen der Furcht
               und der Angst
        1010. Der verschiedene Ursprung von Furcht und
               Angst
S.345   1011. Die Zeitlichkeit von Stimmungen und Affek-
               ten besonders die der Hoffnung
        1012. Die Zeitlichkeit der fahlen Ungestimmt-
               heit der Gleichgültigkeit und ihre Ab-
               grenzung vom Gleichmut
S.346   1013. Gleichgültigkeit und Affektion

c) Die Zeitlichkeit des Verfallens (S.346-349)

S.346   1014. Gegenwart und Verfallen
        1015. Die Neugier als Unverweilen und die Zer-
               streuung
S.347   1016. Der Unterschied von Aufenthaltslosigkeit
               und Augenblick
        1017. Der Zusammenhang von dem "der Gegenwart
               Entspringen" und dem Vergessen
        1018. Die Charaktere des Verfallens und der Zei-
               tigungsmodus des Entspringen der Gegen-
               wart
S.348   1019. Der Ursprung des "Entspringens" der Ge-
               genwart

126

(b) The Temporality of State-of-mind
     (pp.389-396)

p.389   1000. State-of-mind and thrownness
p.390   1001a/b Having been [beenhood] as temporal
                   constitution of the moods
         1002. Methodical considerations about the
               existential-temporal constitution of
               moods
p.391   1003. Fear as bewildered making-present, and
               temporalizing of fear based upon for-
               getting
p.392   1004. The temporality of fear as a forgetting
               which awaits and makes present
p.393   1005. Anxiety as being anxious in the face of
               the "nothing" of the world
         1006. Having been [beenhood] as the temporal
               constitution of anxiety, and the insig-
               nificance which is disclosed by anxiety
p.394   1007. The distinction between fear and anxiety
         1008. The peculiar temporality of anxiety, and
               the possibility of the authentic poten-
               tiality-for-Being
p.395   1009. Anxiety and fear as moods which deter-
               mine themselves in terms of one peculiar
               understanding
         1010. The different sources of fear and anxi-
               ety
         1011. The temporality of moods and affects,
               especially of the phenomenon of hope
p.396   1012. The distinction between the temporality
               of the pallid lack of mood of indiffer-
               ence and equanimity
         1013. Temporality and affection

(c) Temporality and Falling   (pp.396-400)

p.396   1014. The Present and falling
p.397   1015. Curiosity as not-tarrying, and distrac-
               tion
p.398   1016. The distinction between never-dwelling-
               anywhere and the moment of vision
         1017. The connection between the leaping-away
               of the Present and the forgetting
p.399   1018. The characteristics of falling, and the
               mode of temporalizing of the Present's
               leaping-away
         1019. The source of the leaping-away of the
               Present

127

S.348   1020. Geworfenheit, Faktizität des Seins und
              endliche Zeitlichkeit
         1021. Dasein, Geworfenheit und Gegenwart

         d) Die Zeitlichkeit der Rede   (S.349-350)

S.349   1022. Die Rede und die volle Erschlossenheit
              des Da
         1023. Das Problem der existenzial-zeitlichen
              Struktur der Aktionsarten und die Rede
S.350   1024. Das volle Sich-Zeitigen der Zeitlichkeit
              und die Ekstasen
         1025. Charakterisierung der Zeitlichkeit
         1026. Die existenziellen Grundmöglichkeiten
              des Daseins und ihre Fundierung in der
              Zeitlichkeit

              69. Die Zeitlichkeit des
       In-der-Welt-seins und das Problem der
         Transzendenz der Welt (S.350-366)

S.350   1027. Die ekstatische Zeitlichkeit und die
              Strukturen des Daseins
S.351   1028. Methodische Erwägungen:
              1. Über den Zusammenhang von In-der-Welt-
              sein, Sorge und Zeitlichkeit
         1029. 2. Über die ontologische Exposition des
              Problems der Analyse der Zeitlichkeit
              des Besorgens und das Problem der
              Transzendenz

         a) Die Zeitlichkeit des umsichtigen Besorgens
            (S.352-356)

S.352   1030. Der Zusammenhang von Besorgen als Seins-
              art des Daseins und Besorgtem als inner-
              weltlich Zuhandenem
S.353   1031. Bewendenlassen im Sinne von verstehendem
              Entwerfen von Bewandtnis als existenziale
              Struktur des Besorgens
         1032. Bewendenlassen und einfachste Handhabung
              eines Zeugs im Zusammenhang mit dem spe-
              zifisch hantierenden Gegenwärtigen des
              Zeugs

p.399   1020. Thrownness, facticity of Dasein, and
              finite temporality

p.400   1021. Dasein, thrownness, and the Present

(d) The Temporality of Discourse (pp.400-401)

p.400   1022. Discourse, and the full disclosedness of
              the "there"

        1023. The problem of the existential-temporal
              structure of the phenomena of language,
              and discourse

p.401   1024. The full temporalizing of temporality,
              and ecstases

        1025. The characterization of temporality

        1026. The basic existentiell possibilities of
              Dasein, and their being founded in tem-
              porality

69. The Temporality of
Being-in-the-world and the Problem of
the Transcendence of the World
(pp.401-418)

p.401   1027. The ecstatical unity of temporality and
              the structure of Dasein

p.402   1028. Methodical considerations:
              1. About the interconnection of Being-
              in-the-world, care, and temporality

        1029. 2. About the ontological exposition of
              the problem of the analysis of the
              temporality of circumspective concern
              and the problem of the transcendence
              of the world

(a) The Temporality of Circumspective Concern
(pp.403-408)

p.403   1030. The connection between concern as a kind
              of Being of Dasein and that with which
              we concern ourselves as something ready-
              to-hand within-the-world

p.404   1031. Letting-things-be-involved in the sense
              of projecting involvement understanding-
              ly as existential structure of concern

        1032. Letting-things-be-involved and the sim-
              plest handling of items of equipment in
              connection with the specifically manipu-
              lative way in which equipment is made
              present

S.353   1033. Das sich in der Zeitlichkeit gründende
Bewendenlassen und das sich umsichtig
bewegende Besorgen

S.354   1034. Die Zeitlichkeit des Bewendenlassens und
das damit verbundene spezifische Verges-
sen

           1035. Auffälligkeit, Aufdringlichkeit sowie
Aufsässigkeit als Modi des umsichtigen
Begegnenlassens und die Unzufälligkeit
des "objektiv" Vorfindlichen bei der Begegnung des zuhandenen Zeugs

           1036. Das Gegründetsein des Bewendenlassens in
der ekstatischen Einheit des gegenwärti-
gend-behaltenden Gegenwärtigens

S.355   1037. Die zeitliche Struktur des Vermissens

           1038. Die zeitliche Struktur des Überrascht-
werdens

           1039. Das Unbehalten als die zeitliche Struk-
tur des Sich-abfindens

S.356   1040. Widerständigkeit, ekstatische Zeitlichkeit des Besorgens und das Sich-Verste-
hen des faktischen Daseins in seiner
Überlassenheit an eine "Welt"

           1041. Methodische Erwägungen über die bisheri-
ge Untersuchung des durch die Zeitlich-
keit fundierten Bewendenlassens des Besorgens

           b) Der zeitliche Sinn der Modifikation des um-
sichtigen Besorgens zum theoretischen Ent-
decken des innerweltlich Vorhandenen
(S.356-364)

S.356   1042. Methodische Erwägungen:
                1. Über den existenzialen Begriff der
Wissenschaft

S.357   1043. 2. Über die Ausarbeitung von Abschnitt
69b

           1044. Die theoretische Haltung der Wissen-
schaft als Weise des In-der-Welt-seins
und das Problem einer rein geistigen Tä-
tigkeit

S.358   1045. Anschauung als übliches Leitelement aller Interpretation der Erkenntnis in der
bisherigen Geschichte der Philosophie

p.405 1033. Letting-things-be-involved as based upon temporality and the circumspectively operating concern

1034. Letting-things-be-involved which is based upon temporality and the forgetting which is specifically connected with letting-things-be-involved

1035. Conspicuousness, obstrusiveness, and obstinacy as modes of circumspectively letting something be encountered, and the inconspicuousness of what we came across objectively in encountering equipment ready-to-hand

p.406 1036. Letting-things-be-involved and its Being grounded in the ecstatical unity of the making-present which awaits and retains

1037. The temporal structure of "missing-something"

p.407 1038. The temporal structure of the getting-surprised

1039. The non-retaining as the temporal structure of resigning-oneself-to-something

1040. That which exists, ecstatical temporality of concern, and factical Dasein's understanding of itself in its abandonment to a world

p.408 1041. Methodical considerations about the investigation undertaken thus far which dealt with concern as one's letting-things-be-involved that is based upon temporality

b) The Temporal Meaning of the Way in which Circumspective Concern becomes Modified into the Theoretical Discovery of the Present-at-hand Within-the-world (pp.408-415)

p.408 1042. Methodical considerations:
1. About the existential conception of science

1043. 2. About the way in which section 69b will be worked out

p.409 1044. The theoretical attitude of science as a way of Being-in-the-world, and the problem of a purely intellectual activity

1045. Intuition as the customary guiding element of all interpretation of knowledge in the whole course of the history of philosophy

S.359   1046. Gegenwärtigung als existenzialer Sinn
des Näherbringens der Umwelt in der umsichtigen Überlegung

1047. Die umsichtige Gegenwärtigung als mehr-
fach fundiertes Phänomen

S.360   1048. Der existenzial-ontologische Zusammenhang von der Als-Struktur und dem Phäno-
men des Entwurfs

1049. Methodische Erwägungen über den weiteren
Verlauf der Untersuchung

1050. Konkretes Beispiel zur Erläuterung über
umsichtiges Überlegen und theoretisches
Verhalten

S.361   1051. Der Umschlag des Verstehens von Zuhandenem zu Vorhandenem als theoretisches
Verhalten

1052. Theoretisches Verhalten und Entschränkung des Seienden der Umwelt

S.362   1053. Die Entschränkung der Umwelt als Umgrenzung der Region des Vorhandenen

1054. Die Entstehung der mathematischen Physik
und der volle existenziale Begriff der
Wissenschaft

S.363   1055. Die ausgezeichnete Gegenwärtigung als
Charakter des objektivierenden Seins bei
innerweltlich Vorhandenem

1056. Objektivierung und Transzendenz

S.364   1057. Dasein und die damit verbundene Erschlossenheit der Welt

c) Das zeitliche Problem der Transzendenz der
Welt   (S.364-366

S.364   1058. Die Bedeutsamkeit und das Problem der ontologischen Möglichkeit der Welt in ihrer
Einheit mit dem Dasein

1059. Das Dasein und sein primäres Selbstverständnis

1060. Die Horizont habenden Schemata von Zukunft, Gewesenheit und Gegenwart und die
existenzial-zeitliche Bedingung der Möglichkeit der Welt

S.365   1061. Die ekstatische Einheit der Zeitlichkeit
als Grund für die Einheit der Horizont
habenden Schemata von Zukunft, Gewesenheit und Gegenwart

p.410   1046. Making present as existential meaning of
              bringing the environment into circum-
              spective deliberation
p.411   1047. Circumspective making-present as a phe-
              nomenon with more than one kind of
              foundation
         1048. The existential-ontological connection
              between the as-structure and the phenom-
              enon of projection
p.412   1049. Methodical considerations about continu-
              ing the investigation under considera-
              tion
         1050. A concrete example for the explaining of
              circumspective deliberation and of theo-
              retical attitude
         1051. The theoretical attitude as a changing
              from understanding something as ready-
              to-hand to something as present-at-hand
p.413   1052. The theoretical attitude and releasing
              the entities of the confinement to their
              environment
         1053. The releasing from environmental confine-
              ment as delimitation of the region of
              the present-at-hand
         1054. The rise of mathematical physics and the
              full existential conception of science
p.414   1055. The distinctive kind of making-present
              as character of Being which objectifies
              and which is alongside the present-at-
              hand within-the-world
p.415   1056. Objectifying and transcendence
         1057. Dasein and the Being-disclosed to the
              world which is connected with Dasein

    (c) The Temporal Problem of the Transcendence
        of the World   (pp.415-418)

p.415   1058. Signification and the problem of the on-
              tological possibility of the world in
              its unity with Dasein
p.416   1059. Dasein and its primary understanding of
              itself
         1060. The horizonal schemata for future, having
              been [beenhood], and the Present and the
              existential-temporal condition for the
              possibility of the world
         1061. The ecstatical unity of temporality as
              basis for the horizonal schemata of fu-
              ture, Present, and having been [beenhood]

133

S.365   1062. Das Sich-zeitigen der Welt in der Zeit-
                  lichkeit
           1063. Die Welt als Vorausgesetztes bei faktisch
                  besorgendem Sein bei Zuhandenem, bei der
                  Thematisierung des Vorhandenen und bei
                  der Forschung der Wissenschaft
S.366   1064. Der Rückgang auf die ekstatisch-horizon-
                  tal fundierte Transzendenz der Welt als
                  Antwort auf das Transzendenzproblem
           1065. Subjekt, Objekt und Welt
           1066. Methodische Erwägungen über die konkrete
                  Ausarbeitung der Weltstruktur überhaupt

70. Die Zeitlichkeit der
daseinsmässigen Räumlichkeit
(S.367-369)

S.367   1067. Methodische Erwägungen über daseinsmässi-
                  ge Räumlichkeit in Verbindung mit der
                  Zeitlichkeit
           1068. Das Problem der Interpretation der räum-
                  lich-zeitlichen Bestimmtheit des Daseins
           1069. Räumlichkeit des Daseins und Spielraum
                  als Sicheinräumen des Daseins
S.368   1070. Das Sicheinräumen des Daseins und das
                  sichausrichtende Entdecken der Gegend
S.369   1071. Dasein und sein ekstatisch eingenommener
                  Raum als geöffneter Spielraum des Umkrei-
                  ses des nächstbesorgten Zeugganzen
           1072. Die daseinsmässige Räumlichkeit und das
                  Verfallen als wesenhafte Struktur der
                  Sorge
           1073. Die ekstatisch-horizontale Zeitlichkeit
                  als Grund für die Ermöglichung des Ein-
                  bruchs des Daseins in den Raum

71. Der zeitliche Sinn der
Alltäglichkeit des Daseins (S.370-372)

S.370   1074. Methodische Erwägungen:
                  1. Bezüglich der Gründe für die anfäng-
                  liche Orientierung der Analytik des
                  Daseins an der Alltäglichkeit des Da-
                  seins
           1075. 2. Über die Umgrenzung des existenzialen
                  Sinnes der Alltäglichkeit
           1076. Kennzeichnung des Wie der Alltäglichkeit

p.417 1062. The world's temporalizing in temporality
        1063. The world as something which is already
            presupposed in one's Being alongside the
            ready-to-hand concernfully and factical-
            ly, in one's thematizing of the present-
            at-hand, and in scientific research
        1064. The recourse to the transcendence of the
            world -- a transcendence with an ecstat-
            ico-horizonal foundation -- as answer to
            the problem of transcendence
p.418 1065. Subject, object, and world
        1066. Methodical considerations about a con-
            crete working out of the world-structure
            in general

      70. The Temporality of the Spatiality
        that is Characteristic of Dasein
             (pp.418-421)

p.418 1067. Methodical considerations about Dasein's
            spatiality in relation to temporality
        1068. The problem of interpreting Dasein's
            having a spatio-temporal character
p.419 1069. Dasein's spatiality, and leeway as Da-
            sein's having-made-room-for-itself
        1070. Dasein's having-made-room-for-itself and
            the self-directive discovery of a region
p.420 1071. Dasein and the room it has taken in ec-
            statically as an opened leeway of that
            equipmental totality with which it is
            most closely concerned
        1072. Dasein's spatiality, and falling as the
            essential structure of care
p.421 1073. Ecstatico-horizonal temporality as basis
            for Dasein's being enabled to break into
            space

      71. The Temporal Meaning of Dasein's
        Everydayness (pp.421-423)

p.421 1074. Methodical considerations:
          1. Concerning the reasons why at the
            very start the orientation of the
            analytic of Dasein was towards Da-
            sein's everydayness
        1075. 2. About the delimitation of the exis-
            tential meaning of everydayness
p.422 1076. Characterization of the "how" of every-
            dayness

135

S.370   1077. Alltäglichkeit als Behagen in der Gewohn-
                heit
S.371   1078. Alltäglichkeit und die Befindlichkeit
                der fahlen Unbestimmtheit
         1079. Das existenzial-ontologisch Rätselhafte
                des in der faktischen Ausgelegtheit des
                Daseins ontisch Bekannten
         1080. Methodische Erwägungen:
                1. Über die bisherigen Ausführungen be-
                züglich der Struktur der Alltäglich-
                keit
         1081. 2. Über die mögliche zureichende begriff-
                liche Umgrenzung der Alltäglichkeit

                        Kapitel 5

         ZEITLICHKEIT UND GESCHICHTLICHKEIT
                    (S.372-404)

             72. Die existenzial-ontologische
         Exposition des Problems der Geschichte
                     (S.372-377)

S.372   1082. Zusammenfassung über die bisherige Ausar-
                beitung des Zieles der existenzialen Ana-
                lytik
         1083. Erwägungen über die Aufhellung der Zeit-
                lichkeit als ursprünglicher Bedingung
                der Möglichkeit der Sorge
         1084. Methodische Erwägungen:
                1. Über die bisherige einseitige Explika-
                tion des Daseins
S.373   1085. 2. Über den Ansatz für die weitere Ausar-
                beitung der Grundlagen der existenzia-
                len Analytik
         1086. Leben und Tod verstanden als Sein eines
                verharrend-wechselnden Zusammenhanges
                von Erlebnissen
S.374   1087. Die Unmöglichkeit der Durchführung einer
                Analyse der Erstreckung des Daseins zwi-
                schen Geburt und Tod
         1088. Das Problem der vulgären Auffassung des
                Lebenszusammenhanges
         1089. Das Sein des Daseins als Erstreckung sei-
                nes eigenen Seins
         1090. Bewegtheit der Existenz als Geschehen und
                das Problem der Gewinnung eines ontologi-
                schen Verständnisses der Geschichtlichkeit

p.422   1077. Everydayness as comfortableness of the
                accustomed
          1078. Everydayness and the state-of-mind of a
                pallid lack of mood
p.423   1079. The existential-ontological enigma of
                that which is ontically so familiar in
                the way Dasein has been factically in-
                preted
          1080. Methodical considerations:
                1. Of the discussion which has been car-
                ried out until now concerning the
                structure of everydayness
          1081. 2. About a possible adequate conceptual
                delimitation of everydayness

                    Chapter V

          TEMPORALITY AND HISTORICALITY
                 (pp.424-455)

72. Existential-ontological Exposition
of the Problem of History (pp.424-429)

p.424   1082. Summary of the preceding analysis about
                the goal of the existential analysis
          1083. Considerations about casting light upon
                temporality as primordial condition for
                the possibility of care
          1084. Methodical considerations:
                1. About the preceding one-sided expli-
                cation of Dasein
p.425   1085. 2. About the continuing working out of
                the foundations for the existential
                analytic
          1086. Life and death understood as a context
                of experiences which change and persist
p.426   1087. The impossibility to carry out an analy-
                sis of Dasein's stretching-along between
                birth and death
          1088. The problem of the ordinary way of un-
                derstanding the connectedness of life
          1089. Dasein's Being as the stretching-along
                of its own Being
p.427   1090. The movement of existence as historizing
                and the problem of achieving an ontolog-
                ical understanding of historicality

S.375   1091. Methodische Erwägungen:
                1. Über den Zusammenhang von Selbstän-
                   digkeit, Analyse des Geschehens und
                   der Zeitigung als solcher
          1092. 2. Über das Problem der Geschichte als
                   möglichen Gegenstand der Historie
          1093. Kennzeichnung des Weges zur Aufhellung
               der Geschichtlichkeit:
S.376   1094. 1. Kennzeichnung der vulgären Begriffe
                   der Geschichte
          1095. 2. Der Leitfaden für die existenziale
                   Konstruktion der Geschichtlichkeit
          1096. 3. Die existenzielle Möglichkeit einer
                   ausdrücklichen Erschliessung und Er-
                   fassung von Geschichte
          1097. 4. Die Zeitlichkeit des Seins des Da-
                   sein's als Grund für seine Geschicht-
                   lichkeit
          1098. 5. Geschichtlichkeit und Innerzeitigkeit
S.377   1099. Der ontologische Ort der Geschichtlich-
               keit und die Forschungen Wilhelm Diltheys
          1100. Gliederung der Ausarbeitung des existen-
               zialen Problems der Geschichtlichkeit

        73. Das vulgäre Verständnis der
  Geschichte und das Geschehen des Daseins
            (S.378-382)

S.378   1101. Die Einsatzstelle für die existenziale
               Konstruktion der Geschichtlichkeit
          1102. Die Mehrdeutigkeit des Terminus "Ge-
               schichte":
               1. Abgrenzung von Geschichte und Historie
          1103. 2. Geschichte als Vergangenheit im Sinne
                   des Vergangenen
          1104. 3. Geschichte als Herkunft aus der Ver-
                   gangenheit
S.379   1105. 4. Geschichte als Kultur im Sinne des
                   von der Natur unterschiedenen Ganzen
                   des Seienden, das sich in der Zeit
                   wandelt
          1106. 5. Geschichte als das Überlieferte als
                   solches
          1107. Zusammenfassung über das vulgäre Ver-
               ständnis von Geschichte
          1108. Methodische Erwägungen:
               1. Über den Geschehenscharakter von ge-
               schichtlichen Ereignissen

p.427   1091. Methodical considerations:
                1. About the interconnectedness of self-
                constancy, the analysis of historiz-
                ing, and temporalizing as such
         1092. 2. About the problem of history as pos-
                sible object of historiology
p.428   1093. Characterization of the way for casting
                light on historicality:
         1094. 1. Characterization of the ordinary con-
                ception of history
         1095. 2. The clue for construing historicality
                existentially
         1096. 3. The existentiell possibility of dis-
                closing history explicitly and getting
                it in our grasp
         1097. 4. The temporality of Dasein's Being as
                basis for its historicality
p.429   1098. 5. Historicality and within-time-ness
         1099. The ontological locus of the problem of
                historicality and the researches of Wil-
                helm Dilthey
         1100. The main themes of the investigation of
                the problem of historicality

         73. The Ordinary Understanding of
         History, and Dasein's Historizing
                (pp.429-434)

p.429   1101. The right position for construing histor-
                icality existentially
p.430   1102. The various significations of the term
                "history":
                1. The distinction between historical
                actuality and the science of history
         1103. 2. History as something past
         1104. 3. History as derivation from that which
                is past
         1105. 4. History as culture in the sense of
                that totality of entities which is
                distinguished from Nature and which
                changes in time
p.431   1106. 5. History as such which has been handed
                to us as such
         1107. Summary of the ordinary understanding of
                history
         1108. Methodical considerations:
                1. About the historizing character of
                events

139

S.379   1109. 2. Über die Vergangenheit als Ansatz für die weiteren Untersuchungen

S.380   1110. Vorläufige Analyse des der Geschichte angehörigen Zeugs:
                 1. Vergangenes als "Vergangenheit" des Daseins und die Welt

          1111. 2. Da-gewesen-sein des Daseins und Vergangenheit

S.381   1112. Zusammenfassung über das der Geschichte angehörige Zeug

          1113. Das Welt-geschichtliche als das geschichtlich Sekundäre

          1114. Ergebnis der Analyse des geschichtlichen Charakters eines noch vorhandenen Zeugs

S.382   1115. Methodische Erwägungen über das menschliche Dasein als primäres "Subjekt" der Geschichte

74. Die Grundverfassung der Geschichtlichkeit (S.382-387)

S.382   1116. Methodische Erwägungen:
                 1. Über die Durchführung von Abschnitt 74

          1117. 2. Über das Problem des Ursprungs der Möglichkeiten, auf die sich das Dasein faktisch entwirft

S.383   1118. Geworfenheit des Daseins als dem Dasein selbst und seinem Seinkönnen überantwortet-sein

          1119. Die ergriffene Endlichkeit der Existenz und ihr Zurückbringen des Daseins in die Einfachheit seines Schicksals

S.384   1120. Schicksal als das in der eigentlichen Entschlossenheit liegende ursprüngliche Geschehen des Daseins

          1121. Schicksal, Geschick und eigentliches Geschehen des Daseins

S.385   1122. Die Sorge und die Möglichkeit eines im Modus des Schicksals existierenden Seins eines Seienden

          1123. Die Ermöglichung des Schicksals durch eigentliche Zeitlichkeit

          1124. Wiederholung als Modus der sich überliefernden Entschlossenheit und das Schicksal

S.386   1125. Der verborgene Grund der Geschichtlichkeit des Daseins

          1126. Zusammenfassung über Schicksal, Geschick und Wiederholung

p.431   1109. 2. About the past as point of departure for the investigations which will follow

1110. Provisional analysis of the equipment which belongs to history:
1. That which is past as the past of Dasein, and the world

p.432   1111. 2. Dasein's having-been-there and the past

1112. Summary of the equipment which belongs to history

p.433   1113. The world-historical as that which is secondarily historical

1114. Results of the analysis about that historical character of equipment which is still present-at-hand

1115. Methical considerations about human Dasein as primary "subject" of history

74. The Basic Constitution of Historicality (pp.434-439)

p.434   1116. Methical considerations:
1. About the investigation of the subject matter in section 74

1117. 2. About the problem of the source of the possibilities upon which Dasein factically projects itself

p.435   1118. Thrownness of Dasein as Dasein's having been delivered over to itself and to its potentiality-for-Being

1119. The finitude of one's existence which one has grasped and which brings Dasein back into the simplicity of its fate

p.436   1120. Fate as primordial historizing of Dasein which lies in authentic resoluteness

1121. Fate, destiny, and Dasein's authentic historizing

1122. Care and the possibility of that Being of an entity which exists in the mode of fate

p.437   1123. Proposition about fate as Being enabled by authentic temporality

1124. Repetition as a mode of that resoluteness which hands itself down, and fate

p.438   1125. The hidden basis of Dasein's historicality

1126. Summary of fate, destiny, and repetition

141

S.386   1127. Methodische Erwägungen:
                1. Über das Kennzeichen der eigentlichen
                   Geschichtlichkeit des Daseins und die
                   damit verbundenen Probleme
S.387   1128. 2. Über das zunächst zu untersuchende
                   Problem der uneigentlichen Geschicht-
                   lichkeit des Daseins

         75. Die Geschichtlichkeit des Daseins
            und die Weltgeschichte (S.387-392)

S.387   1129. Das Daseinsverständnis der alltäglichen
               Verständigkeit und das Problem seines
               Zusammenhanges mit dem Geschehen der Ge-
               schichte
S.388   1130. Geschichtlichkeit des Daseins und der on-
               tologisch verstandene Ausdruck des Welt-
               Geschichtlichen
S.389   1131. Das je schon "objektiv" daseiende Welt-
               Geschichtliche im Geschehen des existie-
               renden In-der-Welt-seins
         1132. Der Verständnishorizont der uneigentli-
               chen Geschichtlichkeit und der Daseins-
               zusammenhang
S.390   1133. Der Ursprung der Frage nach der Einheit
               der Verkettung der Erlebnisse zwischen
               Geburt und Tod
         1134. Die eigentliche Geschichtlichkeit und
               die in ihr liegende Erstrecktheit der
               ganzen Existenz
S.391   1135. Die Entschlossenheit des Selbst und die
               Stätigkeit der Existenz
         1136. Der Unterschied zwischen uneigentlicher
               und eigentlicher Geschichtlichkeit
S.392   1137. Die existenziale Interpretation der Ge-
               schichtlichkeit und die Rätsel des Seins
               sowie der Bewegung

         76. Der existenziale Ursprung der
         Historie aus der Geschichtlichkeit
               des Daseins (S.392-397)

S.392   1138. Methodische Erwägungen:
                1. Über die ontologische Möglichkeit der
                   Wissenschaften aus der Seinsverfas-
                   sung des Daseins

142

p.438   1127. Methodical considerations:
              1. About the characterization of Da-
              sein's authentic historicality and
              the problems related to it
p.439   1128. 2. About the problem of Dasein's inau-
              thentic historicality which shall
              first be investigated

         75. Dasein's Historicality and
         World-history   (pp.439-444)

p.439   1129. Dasein's understanding of itself by
              means of commen sense, and the problem
              of its connectedness with the historiz-
              ing of history
p.440   1130. Dasein's historicality and the ontologi-
              cally understood expression "the world-
              historical"
p.441   1131. The world-historical and its, in every
              case, already objectively Being there
              in the historizing of existing Being-in-
              the-world
         1132. The horizon of the understanding of in-
              authentic historicality, and the con-
              nectedness of Dasein
p.442   1133. The source of the question of the unity
              with which experiences are linked to-
              gether between birth and death
         1134. Authentic historicality and the whole of
              existence stretched along
p.443   1135. Resoluteness of the Self and the steadi-
              ness of existence
         1136. The distinction between inauthentic and
              authentic historicality
p.444   1137. The existential interpretation of his-
              toricality and the enigmas of Being and
              motion

         76. The Existential Source of
         Historiology in Dasein's Historicality
              (pp.444-449)

p.444   1138. Methodical considerations:
              1. About the ontological possibility of
              all the sciences which is rooted in
              Dasein's constitution of Being

143

S.392   1139. 2. Über das der Geschichtlichkeit des Daseins Verhaftetsein jeder Wissen-
schaft
          1140. 3. Über das ontologische Entwerfen der
Idee der Historie aus der Geschicht-
lichkeit des Daseins
S.393   1141. Die Idee der Historie als Wissenschaft
und die primäre Konstituierung jeder
Wissenschaft durch die Thematisierung
          1142. Die Geschichtlichkeit des Seins des Da-
seins als Offensein in seiner Gewesenheit
S.394   1143. Die Voraussetzung der Geschichtlichkeit
des Historikers bei der Beschaffung,
Sichtung und Sicherung des historischen
Materials
          1144. Der "eigentliche" Gegenstand der Historie:
1. Entwerfung dagewesenen Seins auf seine
eigenste Existenzmöglichkeit
          1145. 2. Das "tatsächlich" eigentlich Dagewe-
sene als die existenzielle Möglichkeit,
in der sich Schicksal, Geschick und
Welt-Geschichte faktisch bestimmen
S.395   1146. 3. Das Sich-aus-der-Zukunft-zeitigen
der historischen Erschliessung
          1147. Ablehnung einer "Allgemeingültigkeit"
der Mass-stäbe als mögliches Kriterium
der Wahrheit in der eigentlichen Historie
          1148. Die Orientierung an den Tatsachen in der
Historie und die Bedeutsamkeit der Über-
lieferungsgeschichte für die Historie
S.396   1149. Die Fragwürdigkeit der Herrschaft des
Historismus
          1150. Friedrich Nietzsche und seine Entdeckung
des Vorgezeichnetseins der Dreifachheit
der Historie in der Geschichtlichkeit des
Daseins
          1151. Die Dreifachheit der Historie und die
Zeitlichkeit
S.397   1152. Eigentliche Erschlossenheit der ge-
schichtlichen Existenz und historische
Wahrheit

144

p.444   1139. 2. About the principle that every factical science is in the grip of histor-
izing
            1140. 3. About projecting ontologically the
idea of Dasein's historicality as the
existential source of historiology
p.445   1141. The idea of historiology as a science,
and the principle that every science is
constituted primarily by thematizing
            1142. Dasein's Being-historical as Being-open
in its character of having been [been-
hood]
p.446   1143. The presupposition of the historicality
of the historian's existence when he ac-
quires, sifts, and secures historical
material
            1144. The "real" object of historiology:
1. Projecting the Dasein which has been
there upon its ownmost possibility of
existence
            1145. 2. That which authentically has been
there as the existentiell possibility
in which fate, destiny, and world-
history have been factically determined
            1146. 3. Historiological disclosure temporal-
izing itself in terms of the future
p.447   1147. Rejection of a universal validity of
standards as possible criterion of truth
in authentic historiology
            1148. Historiology taking its orientation from
the facts and the significance of tradi-
tion history for historiology
p.448   1149. The dubiousness of the dominance of his-
toricism
            1150. Friedrich Nietzsche and his discovery
that the threefold character of historiology is adumbrated in the historicality
of Dasein
            1151. The threefold character of historiology
and temporality
p.449   1152. Authentic disclosedness of historical
existence and historiological truth

77. Der Zusammenhang der vorstehenden Exposition des Problems der Geschichtlichkeit mit den Forschungen Wilhelm Diltheys und den Ideen des Grafen Yorck (S.397-404)

S.397   1153. Die Ideen Wilhelm Diltheys, des Grafen Yorck und Martin Heideggers

        1154. Die bisherige oberflächliche Ansicht über Wilhelm Diltheys Werk

S.398   1155. Zusammenfassung über die Forschungsarbeit Wilhelm Diltheys

        1156. Wilhelm Diltheys Beschäftigung mit der Wissenschaftstheorie

        1157. Methodische Erwägungen über das gemeinsame Interesse bei Wilhelm Dilthey und dem Grafen Yorck

S.399   1158. Die Aufgaben der Erkenntnistheorie und der Methodenlehre erläutert vom Grafen Yorck an der naturwissenschaftlichen Psychologie

        1159. Die Notwendigkeit der Differenzierung zwischen Ontischem und Historischem als Forderung des Grafen Yorck

S.400   1160. Die rein okularen Bestimmungen der traditionellen Geschichtsforschung

        1161. Die Ansicht des Grafen Yorck bezüglich der Fragwürdigkeit der sogenannten Historischen Schule

        1162. Die scharfe Kritik des Grafen Yorck an dem naturwissenschaftlich orientierten Geschichtsverständnis "moderner" Wissenschaft

S.401   1163. Die Basis der Einsicht für den Grafen Yorck in den Grundcharakter der Geschichte als "Virtualität"

S.402   1164. Der Versuch des Grafen Yorck bezüglich der Kategorie des Historischen und eines angemessenen wissenschaftlichen Verständnisses des Lebens

S.403   1165. Das fundamentale Ziel der "Lebensphilosophie" bei dem Grafen Yorck und die Notwendigkeit einer grundsätzlichen Radikalisierung dieser Fragestellung

        1166. Der Zusammenhang von Martin Heideggers vorbereitender existenzial-zeitlichen Analytik des Daseins mit den Ideen des Grafen Yorck und dem Werk Wilhelm Diltheys

77. The Connection of the Foregoing
    Exposition of the Problem of
Historicality with the Researches of
   Wilhelm Dilthey and the Ideas of
      Count Yorck (pp.449-455)

p.449   1153. The ideas of Wilhelm Dilthey, of Count
               Yorck, and of Martin Heidegger
        1154. The superficial opinion about the work
               of Wilhelm Dilthey which has prevailed
               thus far
p.450   1155. Summary of Wilhelm Dilthey's researches
        1156. Wilhelm Dilthey's interest in the theory
               of science
        1157. Methodical considerations about the com-
               mon interest which Wilhelm Dilthey and
               Count Yorck shared
        1158. The task of the theory of knowledge and
               of a doctrine of method explained by
               Count Yorck by using analytic psychology
p.451   1159. Count Yorck's suggestion of the necessi-
               ty to distinguish between the ontical
               and the historiological
        1160. The purely ocular ways of ascertaining
               in traditional historical research
        1161. Count Yorck's opinion concerning the du-
               biousness of the so-called Historical
               school
p.452   1162. Count Yorck's sharp criticism of "mod-
               ern" science and its understanding of
               history which is based upon that of the
               natural sciences
p.453   1163. "Virtuality" as the basic character of
               history understood as fundamental in-
               sight by Count Yorck
p.454   1164. Count Yorck's attempt to gain a proper
               understanding of the categories of the
               Historical and of a raising up of life
               into the kind of scientific understand-
               ing which is appropriate to it
p.455   1165. Count Yorck's insight into the fundamen-
               tal aim of the philosophy of life, and
               the necessity to radicalize in principle
               this formulation of the question
        1166. The connection between Martin Heidegger's
               preparatoty existential-temporal analytic
               of Dasein, the ideas of Count Yorck, and
               the work of Wilhelm Dilthey

147

Kapitel 6

ZEITLICHKEIT UND INNERZEITIGKEIT ALS
URSPRUNG DES VULGÄREN ZEITBEGRIFFES
(S.404-437)

78. Die Unvollständigkeit der
vorstehenden zeitlichen Analyse
des Daseins (S.404-406)

S.404   1167. Methodische Erwägungen über das Konsti-
tuieren des Seins des Daseins durch die
Zeitlichkeit und die faktisch ontisch-
zeitliche Auslegung der Geschichte
1168. Das Problem des faktischen Zeit-"habens"
des Daseins
1169. Methodische Erwägungen über den Zusammenhang von Zeitlichkeit und Weltzeit
S.405   1170. Der vulgäre Zeitbegriff und seine Herkunft
1171. Die Ausbildung des vulgären Zeitbegriffes und der Unterschied der Interpretation der Zeit bei Hegel und Martin Heidegger
S.406   1172. Das Problem des Seins der Zeit und die
Gliederung von Kapitel 6

79. Die Zeitlichkeit des Daseins und
das Besorgen von Zeit (S.406-411)

S.406   1173. Zusammenfassung über das Dasein als umsichtig verständiges Besorgen und dessen
Gründung in der Zeitlichkeit
1174. Die Kennzeichnung von dem Dann, dem Damals und dem Jetzt
S.407   1175. Datierbarkeit als Bezugsstruktur
1176. Das Sich-auslegen des gewärtigend-behal-
tenden Gegenwärtigens als das der Datierbarkeit wesenhaft Zugehörige
S.408   1177. Zeit als das im "Jetzt" angesprochene,
ausgelegte Gegenwärtigen
1178. Datierbarkeit und die ekstatische Einheit
der Zeitlichkeit:
1. Das Gegenwärtigen von Seiendem
1179. 2. Die dem Jetzt, Dann und Damals zuge-
hörigen Horizonte

Chapter VI

TEMPORALITY AND WITHIN-TIME-NESS
AS THE SOURCE OF THE ORDINARY
CONCEPTION OF TIME   (pp.456-488)

78. The Incompleteness of the Foregoing
Temporal Analysis of Dasein (pp.456-458)

p.456   1167. Methodical considerations about consti-
               tuting Dasein's Being by temporality and
               the factical ontico-temporal interpreta-
               tion of history
        1168. The problem of Dasein's factical having-
               the-time
        1169. Methodical considerations about the in-
               terconnectedness of temporality and
               world-time
p.457   1170. The ordinary conception of time and its
               source
        1171. The development of the ordinary concep-
               tion of time and the different ways of
               Hegel's and Martin Heidegger's interpre-
               tation of time
p.458   1172. The problem of the Being of time, and
               the main themes of chapter 6

79. Dasein's Temporality, and our
Concern with Time   (pp.458-464)

p.458   1173. Summary of Dasein as concern of circum-
               spective common sense which is grounded
               in temporality
        1174. The characterization of the "then", the
               "on-the-former-occasion", and the "now"
p.459   1175. Datability as a relational structure
        1176. The making-present which awaits and re-
               tains and which interprets itself as
               that which belongs essentially to data-
               bility
p.460   1177. Time as that making-present which has
               been interpreted and is addressed in the
               "now"
        1178. Datability as the ecstatical unity of
               temporality:
               1. The making-present of entities
p.461   1179. 2. The horizons which belong to the "now",
               the "then", and the "on-that-former-
               occasion"

149

S.409   1180. Gewärtigend-behaltendes Gegenwärtigen
              als Zeitspanne und ihr Erschlossensein
              als ekstatische Erstrecktheit der ge-
              schichtlichen Zeit
        1181. Das Sich-Datieren der Zeit im jeweiligen
              Modus des besorgenden Sich-Zeit-lassens
              und die Verdeckung der Zeit
S.410   1182. Das Wesen der Zeit bei eigentlichem und
              uneigentlichem Existieren
        1183. Die Zeit und das faktisch geworfene Da-
              sein
        1184. Das alltägliche Besorgen und die Öffent-
              lichkeit der Zeit

                    80. Die besorgte Zeit und
              die Innerzeitigkeit (S.411-420)

S.411   1185. Methodische Erwägungen über die Ausarbei-
              tung der Zeitlichkeit des Daseins und
              das Besorgen von Zeit
        1186. Die Veröffentlichung der Zeit im Besorgen
        1187. Zeitrechnung als Horizont eines Besorgens
              der Zeit und die sich in der Zeitrechnung
              zeitigende Veröffentlichung der Zeit
S.412   1188. Die öffentliche Zeit als Innerzeitigkeit
        1189. Sichtmöglichkeit als Notwendigkeit für
              das alltägliche umsichtige In-der-Welt-
              sein und die für das Dasein mit der fak-
              tischen Erschlossenheit seiner Welt ent-
              deckte Natur
        1190. Das der Analyse der natürlichen Zeitrech-
              nung zugrundeliegende "primitive" Dasein:
              1. Die Sonne und das Datieren der Zeit
                 seitens des Daseins aus dem, was im
                 Horizont der Überlassenheit and die
                 Welt innerhalb der Welt begegnet
S.413   1191. 2. Datierung als Rechnen mit der Zeit im
                 Sinne einer Zeitmessung
        1192. 3. Die Sonne als natürlicher Zeitmesser
                 und Uhr
S.414   1193. Methodische Erwägungen über die Ausarbei-
              tung des Problems der in der Zeit-messung
              besorgten Zeit

150

p.461 1180. The making-present which awaits and re-
              tains as span of time, and its disclos-
              edness as the way in which its histori-
              cal temporality has been ecstatically
              stretched along
p.462 1181. Time's dating itself in one's current
              mode of allowing oneself time concern-
              fully, and the covering up of time
p.463 1182. The nature of time in authentic and in-
              authentic existing
       1183. Time and the factically thrown Dasein
       1184. Everyday concern and the publicness of
              time

80. The Time with which we Concern Ourselves, and Within-time-ness
(pp.464-472)

p.464 1185. Methodical considerations about the in-
              vestigation of Dasein's temporality and
              concerning oneself with time
       1186. Time as having-already-made-itself-pub-
              lic in concern
       1187. Time-reckoning as the horizon of a con-
              cern with time, and the making-public
              of time which temporalizes itself in
              time-reckoning
p.465 1188. Public time as within-time-ness
       1189. Possibility of sight as necessity for
              the everyday circumspective Being-in-
              the-world, and Nature which has been un-
              covered for Dasein's factical disclosed-
              ness of its world
       1190. The "primitive" Dasein on which the anal-
              ysis of "natural" time-reckoning is
              based:
              1. The sun, and Dasein's dating of time
                 in terms of something it encounters
                 within the world and within the hori-
                 zon of its abandonment to the world
p.466 1191. 2. Dating as reckoning with time in the
                 sense of measuring time
       1192. 3. The sun as a natural clock
p.467 1193. Methodical considerations about the de-
              lineation of the problem of that time
              with which we are concerned when we
              measure

151

S.414   1194. Die Weltzeit als die in der Zeitigung
                der Zeitlichkeit sich veröffentlichende
                Zeit und struktural vollständige Charak-
                terisierung der besorgten Zeit
S.415   1195. Methodische Erwägungen über Zeitmessung
                und ihr Gegründetsein in der Zeitlich-
                keit des Daseins
          1196. Der Uhrzeuggebrauch:
                1. Des modernen Menschen
          1197. 2. Des archaischen Menschen
S.416   1198. Das Problem der Zeitablesung
          1199. Zeitablesung als wesenhaftes Jetzt-sagen
          1200. Zeitmessung als Vollzug einer Veröffent-
                lichung der Zeit
S.417   1201. Die Zeitlichkeit des Daseins und die an
                einen Raum gebundene Zeit
S.418   1202. Die Datierung der Zeit aus dem "räumlich"
                Vorhandenen als Gegenwärtigen des in je-
                dem Jetzt für jeden vorhandenen Seienden
                in seiner Anwesenheit
          1203. Die Uhr und die sich zeit-nehmende Zeit-
                lichkeit
          1204. Methodische Erwägungen über den Zusammen-
                hang des Uhrgebrauches mit der sich zeit-
                nehmenden Zeitlichkeit
S.419   1205. Die mit der Erschlossenheit von Welt ver-
                öffentlichte Weltzeit
          1206. Die "Objektivität" der Weltzeit
          1207. Die "Subjektivität" der Weltzeit
S.420   1208. Methodische Erwägungen über die weitere
                Ausarbeitung des Themas "Weltzeit"

          81. Die Innerzeitigkeit und die
        Genesis des vulgären Zeitbegriffes
                  (S.420-428)

S.420   1209. Aristoteles Definition der Zeit
S.421   1210. Die im Uhrgebrauch "gesichtete" Weltzeit
                als Jetzt-Zeit
S.422   1211. Das Nacheinander als die vulgäre Ausle-
                gung der Weltzeit
          1212. Die vulgäre Zeitauslegung und ihre nivel-
                lierende Verdeckung der Weltzeit

152

p.467   1194. World-time as the time which makes itself public in the temporalizing of temporality, and the complete structural
characterization of that time with which
we concern ourselves

p.468   1195. Methodical considerations about that
measurement of time which is grounded in
the temporality of Dasein

           1196. The use of clocks:
1. By modern humankind

           1197. 2. By archaic humankind

p.469   1198. The problem of the reading-off-the-time

           1199. Reading-off-the-time as essentially say-
ing "now"

           1200. Measuring time as execution of the making-
public of time

p.470   1201. Temporality of Dasein, and time which is
bound up with a location

           1202. Dating of time in terms of what is spa-
tially present-at-hand as signifying that
an entity which is present-at-hand for
everyone in every "now" is made present
in its own presence

p.471   1203. The clock and that temporality which
takes its time

           1204. Methodical considerations about the con-
nection of the use of clocks with that
temporality which takes its time

           1205. World-time which has been made public
with the disclosedness of the world

           1206. The "objectivity" of world-time

p.472   1207. The "subjectivity" of world time

           1208. Methodical considerations about further
delineating the theme of world-time

81. Within-time-ness and the Genesis
of the Ordinary Conception of Time
(pp.472-480)

p.472   1209. Aristotle's definition of time
p.473   1210. The world-time which is sighted in the
use of clocks as the now-time
p.474   1211. The understanding of world-time as a suc-
cession of "nows"

           1212. The ordinary interpretation of time which
covers up and levels off world-time

153

S.422   1213. Das Fehlen des Horizontes für das Zugäng-
lich-machen-können von Welt, Bedeutsam-
keit und Datierbarkeit bei der Interpretation der Weltzeit als Jetzt-Zeit

S.423   1214. Die Auffassung von der Zeit als Vorhandenem im Sinne der entstehend-vergehen-
den Jetztfolge

1215. Die Auffassung von der Zeit als ununter-
brochener und lückenloser Jetztfolge und
das Verdecktbleiben der spezifischen
Struktur der Weltzeit

S.424   1216. Die These von der "Unendlichkeit" der
Zeit und die Nivellierung von Weltzeit
und Zeitlichkeit

1217. Die Leitung des vulgären Daseinsverständ-
nisses durch das Man als Grund für die
Nivellierung der Weltzeit und für die
Verdeckung der Zeitlichkeit

S.425   1218. Die Rede vom Vergehen der Zeit als Zeichen für ein Verstehen des Daseins bezüglich seiner Zeitlichkeit

S.426   1219. Die Herkunft der öffentlichen Zeit aus
der Zeitlichkeit als Grund für die Unum-
kehrbarkeit der Zeit

1220. Vulgäre Zeitvorstellung, vulgäres Verstehen der Geschichte und die Interpretation
der aus der Zeitlichkeit geschöpften vollen Struktur der Weltzeit

1221. Zeitlichkeit als ursprüngliche Zeit und
ihre Unzugänglichkeit im Horizont des
vulgären Zeitverständnisses

1222. Das Grundphänomen der Zeit bei der eksta-
tisch-horizontalen Zeitlichkeit und bei
dem vulgären Zeitverständnis

S.427   1223. Die vulgäre Zeiterfahrung als Weltzeit
und ihr gleichzeitiger ausgezeichneter
Bezug zu "Seele" und "Geist"

<u>82. Die Abhebung des existenzial-
ontologischen Zusammenhanges von
Zeitlichkeit, Dasein und Weltzeit
gegen Hegels Auffassung der Beziehung
zwischen Zeit und Geist</u> (S.428-436)

S.428   1224. Methodische Erwägungen über die zu unter-
nehmende Untersuchung von Hegels Zeitbe-
griff

p.474   1213. The interpretation of world-time as now-
               time and the absence of a horizon by
               which world, significance, and databili-
               ty can be made accessible to it
p.475   1214. The conception of time as something
               present-at-hand in the sense of a se-
               quence of "nows" constantly arising and
               passing
         1215. The conception of time as a sequence of
               "nows" which is uninterrupted and has no
               gaps, and the specific structure of
               world-time that remains covered up
p.476   1216. The theses that time is infinite, and
               the levelling off of world-time and of
               temporality
         1217. The guidance of that which is ordinarily
               understood by the "they" as the basis
               for the levelling off of world-time and
               the convering-up of temporality
p.477   1218. The talk of time's passing-away as a
               sign of Dasein's understanding of its
               temporality
p.478   1219. The originating of public time in tempo-
               rality as reason for the irreversibility
               of time
         1220. Ordinary representation of time, ordi-
               nary understanding of history, and the
               interpretation of the full structure of
               world-time which has been drawn from tem-
               porality
p.479   1221. Temporality as primordial time and its
               inaccessibility in the horizon of the
               ordinary understanding of time
         1222. The basic phenomenon of time in ecstati-
               co-horizonal temporality and in the or-
               dinary understanding of time
         1223. The ordinary experience of time as world-
               time and its relationship to "soul" and
               "spirit"

         82. A Comparison of the Existential-
      ontological Connection of Temporality,
      Dasein, and World-time, with Hegel's
      Way of Taking the Relation between
         Time and Spirit (pp.480-486)

p.480   1224. Methodical considerations about the in-
               vestigation into Hegel's conception of
               time

155

a) Hegels Begriff der Zeit (S.428-432)

S.428   1225. Die Ontologie der Natur als Kriterium
der leitenden Grundauffassung der Zeit
bei Hegel

S.429   1226. Das Sein des Raumes als Zeit bei Hegel

1227. Der Raum als Punktualität bei Hegel

1228. Hegels Satz von der Wahrheit des Raumes
als Zeit

S.430   1229. Die Zeit als Negation "der Negation als
Punktualität" bei Hegel und ihr Kenn-
zeichen als Jetzt-Punkt

1230. Hegels Bestimmung der Zeit als ange-
schautes Werden und ihr primäres Verstehen aus dem Jetzt

S.431   1231. Hegels Zeitinterpretation als vulgäres
Zeitverständnis

1232. Illustrierung des vulgären Zeitverständnisses durch Zitate aus Hegels Werk

1233. Abschliessende Charakteristik von Hegels
Zeitauffassung

b) Hegels Interpretation des Zusammenhanges
    zwischen Zeit und Geist (S.433-436)

S.433   1234. Hegels Verständnis des Geistes

1235. Der Begriff und das Ich als Allgemein-
heit sowie als Einzenheit bei Hegel

S.434   1236. Das Negieren der Negation und die
Selbstoffenbarung des Geistes bei Hegel

1237. Hegels Ansicht von der Notwendigkeit,
dass der Geist in die Zeit falle

1238. Hegels Ansicht von der Zeit als abstrak-
ter Negativität und von dem Begriff als
Macht der Zeit

S.435   1239. Hegels Ansicht von der Zeit als Vorhandenem, das dem Geist gegenüberstehe

1240. Hegels Anstrengung um ein Begreifen der
Konkretion des Geistes als Ausgangspunkt
für die Konstruktion des Zusammenhanges
von Zeit und Geist

1241. Existieren des Geistes im Sinne der ursprünglichen Zeitigung der Zeitlichkeit
als Martin Heideggers Ansatzpunkt für
den Zusammenhang von Zeit und Geist

(a) Hegel's Conception of Time   (pp.480-484)

p.480   1225. Ontology of Nature as the criterion
        which guides Hegel's basic conception of
        time
p.481   1226. Hegel's idea of the Being of space as
        time
        1227. Space seen as punctuality by Hegel
        (1228) Hegel's proposition about the truth of
        space as time
p.482   1229. Hegel's idea of time as negation of "the
        negation as punctuality" and its charac-
        teristics as now-point
        1230. Hegel's definition of time as "intuited
        becoming" and the resultant primary un-
        derstanding of time in terms of the "now"
p.483   1231. Hegel's interpretation of time as ordi-
        nary understanding of time
        1232. Illustrating Hegel's ordinary understand-
        ing of time by quotes from his own writ-
        ings
        1233. Concluding characteristics of Hegel's
        conception of time

(b) Hegel's Interpretation of the Connection
    between Time and Spirit   (pp.484-486)

p.484   1234. Hegel's understanding of spirit
        1235. Hegel's idea of the concept, and of the
        "I" as universality and individuality
        1236. The negating of the negation and the
        self-manifestation of the spirit
p.485   1237. Hegel's idea of the spirit's necessity
        to fall into time
        1238. Hegel's idea of time as abstract nega-
        tivity, and of the concept as the power
        of time
        1239. Hegel's understanding of time as some-
        thing present-at-hand which gets con-
        trasted with spirit
p.486   1240. Hegel's struggle to conceive the "con-
        cretion" of the Spirit as point of de-
        parture for construing the connection
        between spirit and time
        1241. The existing of the spirit in the sense
        of primordial temporalizing of tempora-
        lity as Martin Heidegger's point of de-
        parture for the connection between time
        and temporality

157

83. Die existenzial-zeitliche Analytik des Daseins und die fundamentalontologische Frage nach dem Sinn von Sein überhaupt
(S. 436-437)

S.436   1242. Ergebnis und Problematik der bisherigen existenzialen Analyse des Daseins

1243. Die ontologische Problematik der Seinsfrage

S.437   1244. Die bisherige Untersuchung und das Problem des Weges zum Ursprung und der Möglichkeit der Idee des Seins überhaupt

1245. Das Ergebnis der existenzialen Analyse des Daseins und die bleibenden, weiterhin zu untersuchenden Probleme der Forschung an der Idee des Seins

83. The Existential-temporal Analytic of Dasein, and the Question of Fundamental Ontology as to the Meaning of Being in General
(pp. 486-488)

p.486   1242. Results and problematics of the existential analytic of Dasein

p.487   1243. The ontological problematic of the question of Being

            1244. The preceding investigations, and the problems of the way to the source and of the possibility of an idea of Being

p.488   1245. Results of the existential analytic of Dasein, and the problems of the research concerning the idea of Being which remain and will continue to be investigated in the time to come